2004 PO

ONCE UPON A RHYME

IMAGINATION FOR A NEW GENERATION

Leeds

Edited by Steve Twelvetree

 Young**Writers**

First published in Great Britain in 2004 by:
Young Writers
Remus House
Coltsfoot Drive
Peterborough
PE2 9JX
Telephone: 01733 890066
Website: www.youngwriters.co.uk

SB ISBN 1 84460 453 5

Foreword

Young Writers was established in 1991 and has been passionately devoted to the promotion of reading and writing in children and young adults ever since. The quest continues today. Young Writers remains as committed to engendering the fostering of burgeoning poetic and literary talent as ever.

This year's Young Writers competition has proven as vibrant and dynamic as ever and we are delighted to present a showcase of the best poetry from across the UK. Each poem has been carefully selected from a wealth of *Once Upon A Rhyme* entries before ultimately being published in this, our twelfth primary school poetry series.

Once again, we have been supremely impressed by the overall high quality of the entries we have received. The imagination, energy and creativity which has gone into each young writer's entry made choosing the best poems a challenging and often difficult but ultimately hugely rewarding task - the general high standard of the work submitted amply vindicating this opportunity to bring their poetry to a larger appreciative audience.

We sincerely hope you are pleased with our final selection and that you will enjoy *Once Upon A Rhyme Leeds* for many years to come.

Contents

Christ Church Upper Armley CE Primary School

Cobden Primary School

Christopher Boyd (10)   36
Kane Hirst (10)   36
Samantha Joyce (8)   37
Holly Bannister (8)   37
Holli Rutter (9)   38
Ryan Gillen (9)   38

Gildersome Primary School
Annie Smith (11)   39
Matthew Cross (10)   39
James Stratton (11)   40
Jenny Bedford (10)   41
Chloe Proctor (10)   42
Stephanie Waddle (11)   42
Abigail Webb (10)   43
Charlotte Smith (10)   43
Kirsten Parry (10)   44
Sophie Morton (10)   44
Jessica Hill (11)   45

Hawksworth CE Primary School
Amy Swales (7)   45
Kristy Fawcett (9)   46
Toby Mountain (9)   47
Amy Turk (8)   48
Elizabeth Heard (8)   49
Charlotte Fisher (8)   50
Ben Swinton (8)   50
Ella Hainsworth-Brear (8)   51
Adam Laycock (8)   51
Amy Hill (9)   52
Claire McFetridge (7)   53
Olivia Armstrong (8)   53
Sophie Whitham (9)   54
Bethany Williamson (7)   54
Emma Pickersgill (8)   55
Daniel Holt (8)   55
Adam Swinton (8)   56
Sarah Tate (8)   56
Louis Barker (7)   57
Claudia Marchbank (7)   57

Katharine Foxton (8)   58
Joseph Mountain (7)   59

Hovingham Primary School
Temur Al-Jihad (8)   59
Sahiba Sajid (7)   60
Max Lee (7)   60
Alisha Liaqat (7)   61
Mehreen Ali (8)   61
Adnan Mohammed (8)   61
Natasha Saeed (8)   62
Aamir Ali (7)   62
Jonathan Brown (8)   63
Moheen Khan (7)   63
Farhana Yasin (8)   64

Lawns Park Primary School
Ashleigh Myers (10)   64
Nathaniel Harrison (9)   65
Amy Robinson (11)   65
Emma McVey (11)   66
Rebekka Danby (9)   66
Kim Taylor (9)   67
Jennifer Rasal (7)   67
Jade Kernick (8)   68
Charlotte Rose Sylvester (8)   68
Tayler-Marie Hackney (8)   68
Ellecia Rose McLoughlin (9)   69
Thomas Needham (8)   69
Ellis Jaques (9)   69
Liberty Wightman (10)   70
Sophie Dickson (9)   70

Leeds Grammar School
Gideon Ziff (11)   71
Felix Hill (11)   72
David Crothers (10)   73
Jack Bickler (10)   74
William Cracknell (11)   74
James Bickler (10)   74
Oliver Lestner (11)   75

Daniel Saffer (11)	76
Zack Sorkin (9)	77
David Lee (10)	78
George Berson (11)	79
Haaris Ahmed (11)	80
Jack Goldstone (11)	80
Samuel Rozday (10)	81
Henry Verhees (10)	81
Harry Fellerman (10)	82
Adnan Memon (11)	82
Tom Wilcox (9)	83
Mark Fuszard (11)	83
James Wainman (11)	84
Joseph Raper (7)	84
Hugo Govett (11)	85
Dominic Brooke (10)	86
Adithya Sreedharan (7)	87
Freddie Machin (7)	87
Adam Ross (7)	87
Henry Richmond (10)	88
Daniel Bello (8)	88
Harmandeep Tatla (9)	89
Max Elgot (7)	89
James Groom (7)	89
James Roberts (8)	90
Marius Tirlea (8)	90
Joel Groom (7)	90
Tim Ruston (8)	91
Toby Ziff (8)	91
Jonathan Castle (9)	92
Henry Dalton (8)	93
Max Rooney (9)	93
Joseph Martin (9)	94
David Swarbrick (9)	94
Christopher Mellor (9)	95
Daniel Davidson (8)	96
George Lestner (8)	96
Edward Pellow (8)	97
Joe Mitchell (9)	97
Oishik Raha (8)	98
Andrew Hooley (9)	98
William Lax (8)	99

Miles Hill Primary School

Our Lady's School

Robert Popple (10)   139
Zoe Lister (10)   140
Tyler Brook (11)   140
Toni Bolton (11)   141
Samantha Thackray (11)   141
Zoe McGettigan (10)   142
Hannah Wakefield (11)   142
Cruise Lister (11)   143

Richmond House School

Ashley Hemingway (10)   143
Fraser Shiels (9)   144
Jessica Lintin (9)   144
James Wilson (10)   145
Jennie Stubbs (9)   145
Henry Cranston (9)   146
Charlotte Barraclough (10)   146
Joe Whitehurst (10)   147
Rayhan Ali (10)   147
Malkit Sihra (9)   148
Nayab Chaudhry (9)   148
Charlotte Denison (9)   149
Andrew Coates (10)   149
Oliver Penn (10)   150
Jessica Wetherop (10)   150
Andrew Ward (11)   151
Rebecca Jackson (9)   151
Barnaby McMahon (11)   152
Charlotte Benstock (9)   152
Oliver Packman (10)   153
Nicholas Winn (7)   153
Eleanor Browne (9)   154
Sherriden Rastegar (9)   154
Molly Hayward (9)   155
Mike Wren-Kirkham (9)   155
Hannah Donkin (9)   156
Katie Parsloe (8)   156
Juliette Izard (9)   156
Daisy Lee (8)   157
Jessica Lloyd (7)   158
Adam Bowie (7)   158

Achese Hector-Goma (7)	179
Andrew Adjei-Doku (8)	179
Athene-Nanette Idiabor-Moses (10)	180
Anujesupo Alabi (9)	180
Adele Elizabeth Johnson (10)	181
Becky Robinson (11)	182
Kirsty Heyes (10)	182
Ben Mowbray (10)	183
Sinead Flanagan (11)	183
Iberedem Udoh (10)	184
Jake Meredith (8)	184
Chelsea Aveyard (8)	185

Swillington Primary School

John Gibson (9)	185
Rachel Curtis (9)	186
Lauren Cheesbrough (9)	186
Lois Jones (8)	187
Hannah Carmichael (8)	187
Luke Monks-Palmer (8)	187
Emma Wallace (9)	188
Jade Linley (8)	188
Chloe Hanlon (9)	188
Charlotte Wallis (8)	189
Emily Waldron (8)	189
Brogan Louise Nugent (8)	190
Rosie Whelan (9)	190
Luke Smith (9)	190
Charlotte Gibson (10)	191
Hugh-Grant Babbage (8)	192
Holly McManus (8)	192

Swinnow Primary School

Christian Hughes (8)	192
Stacey Louise Sharp (7)	192
Emma Urwin (8)	193
Stacey Wade (8)	193
Natasha Hardisty (8)	193
Ashleigh Abbott (10)	193
Charlotte Bell (7)	194
Callum Riley (8)	194

Wakefield Tutorial Prep School

The Poems

Rugby, The Best Game In The World

When I play rugby for my team,
I am simply the best they've ever seen.

See me run, see me pass,
See me tackle anything above the grass.

Watch me fly down the wing to score an ozzie,
And hear the crowd sing.

Scoring tries, kicking goals,
Not that bad for an eight-year-old.

Robbie Williamson (8)
Beecroft Primary School

If You Want To Be Cool

If you want to be cool
Then swim in a pool
But, if you don't want to be a fool
Just go to school.

In school you read,
Write, sing and learn how to plant a seed
Soon you'll be in the lead
And really that's cool.

Bothaina Tashani (8)
Beecroft Primary School

Leeds United

L eeds United are playing Liverpool
E very player is doing their best
E ddy says to Leeds, 'Score a goal'
D efender Kelly kicks the ball
S mith scores the winning goal.

Ghagan Duggal (7)
Beecroft Primary School

Fluffy Black 'What'

I am agile around the abbey,
My fluffy black ears flap as I bounce,
As my black tail swings, wobbly,
My eyes are brown staring
At my scrumptious meat,
I am playful,
I talk for attention,
I speak in a Scottish accent compared to a dog that barks!
What am I?
A dog, a human,
A cat or a rabbit?
Can I really talk?
Which one?
Which one?
Think!
Think!
I am called
Max the dog!

Bejal Mistry (9)
Beecroft Primary School

The River Is . . .

The river is both living and dead
As the living flows down the stream
Over pebbles and under bridges
The dead stays behind
As the living travels up the stream
And gets on with its life
The dead stays behind
Lonely and lost
Like the river let your life flow
Go ahead with the current.

Anna Love (11)
Beecroft Primary School

When Elvis Died

I wish with all my heart
My idol was alive
I listen to his songs each night
He makes my life so bright

If I could have one wish in life
My dreams would all come true
To visit Graceland where he lived
And share his success too

But I will have to settle
For his music's all I have
If only he was still alive
I'd be his biggest fan.

Elle Lynn Brown (8)
Beecroft Primary School

Snow

Snow
Falling gently, silently
Cold and white
Covering houses, gardens, trees
Cold and white
Children building snowmen
Cold and white
They play with snowballs
Cold and white
Everything is
Cold and white
Snow.

Christopher Bradley (9)
Beecroft Primary School

The FA Cup Final

It is the FA Cup final,
The Millennium Stadium is packed up,
Two sets of supporters,
Almost 70,000 fans here.
The teams come out,
A scene of people,
Cheering and enthusiastic,
There is a large cheer when the match kicks off.
It has been a slow, but exciting, 45 minutes and it is still 0-0.
The second half begins with a tense match in the players' hands,
Every player's face determined to lift the famous trophy.
It is injury time,
Still goalless,
Until a penalty is given to the red team,
He runs up,
Every person in the stadium stands up,
Then the striker hits it into the bottom corner of the net.
The whole crowd goes wild,
Finally, the captain lifts up the trophy,
And the crowd claps the players.
It was an exciting game,
It was the best FA Cup final ever.

Lewis Richardson (11)
Beecroft Primary School

Blame

Scolded, banished, punished, weeping,
Why did they blame me?
The open sky above,
And weed for my floor,
He stole matches from my mum,
He set fire to my back garden,
Turned the bedroom key,
Why blame me?

Emma Marks (9)
Beecroft Primary School

My Naughty Little Brother

My naughty little brother is a pain!
He chatters too much
And screams at once.
He will beat me up and strangle me at once,
If I get my way,
If he doesn't get his way.
He is the one who gets the hugs,
He doesn't let me have a hug
But he will let my friends have whatever.
He eats the shop at once,
He is very clever and knows what's going on,
He listens to me when I talk about him.
He will hide my stuff but when I take a step
He will tell me to move.
If I watch TV he will say, 'Why you?'
My naughty little brother.

Priya Lota (9)
Beecroft Primary School

Catherine Wheel

Spark, hiss, whoosh.
The Catherine wheel swizzles into motion.
Colours swirling, sparks jumping,
Light glittering in the dark, wintry night.
The brightness slowly fades
And smoke twirls in the blowing wind.
Wow! The fireworks were beautiful.
I wish it could be Bonfire Night every night!

Amy Parsons (7)
Beecroft Primary School

Untitled

I banged a nail,
I hit my thumb,
My brother laughed,
But not my mum.
My brother tried to paint a space,
The paint went splattering on his face.
He turned around and began to cry,
My mummy laughed and so did I.

Chelsie Kearsley (8)
Beecroft Primary School

The Shark

The shark is the hunter of the sea
Shaped like a torpedo.
He roams the ocean ensnaring his prey.
The powerful creature speeds through the water
Terrorising the tiddlers.
He tears them in half and chews them,
He lies in wait in the shadows
Ready to catch his human prey.

Andrew Bradley (10)
Beecroft Primary School

Rome At Home

Rome is at home today
Because they are leaving tomorrow
It's sad to see them go away
So very sad, very sad
They weren't bad
They built a man
That boiled an egg in the frying pan.

Matthew Bonsell-Stanhope (9)
Beecroft Primary School

The Sunset

T he sun
H appy children playing
E veryone is lively and cheerful

S parkles like a diamond necklace
U pon the turquoise sea
N ight-time falls
S un settles
E verything is colourful red, pink and orange as
T he sun says, 'Goodnight, sleep tight.'

Kirsty Donohoe (10)
Beecroft Primary School

Owl

Owl
Scanned the land for its unlucky victim
Owl targeted its victim
Owl waited, waited
Owl flew off the post it was resting upon
And struck its victim
It captured its prey with razor talons
Owl feasts upon its victims.

Ella Gregson (10)
Beecroft Primary School

Horses

Fast as lightning,
They gallop,
Hooves pounding against the ground like hailstones,
They canter, softly, silently, swiftly through the night,
Becoming slower and slower,
Until stopping fully,
To drink at a nearby creek.

Natalie Smith (9) & Natasha Taylor
Beecroft Primary School

Ice Cream Summer

I t is as hot as the sun,
C hocolate swirling down my arm,
E very summer it tastes better still.

C olours - white, brown, pink, blue,
R each into the ice cream van,
E ating this treat as it drops down my drain,
A scrumptious food for a hot summer's day,
M elting as I run and play.

S un sizzling on a hot day,
U p I go out to play,
M elting your ice cream,
M y mum is washing my clothes,
E ating up my dinner on a summer's day,
R ain comes the next day.

Paramdeep Duggal (9)
Beecroft Primary School

Funky Flowers

F lowers spread,
U pon a blanket of emerald-green,
N icely arranged to make a sea of colours.
K een to be seen, the flowers grow,
Y et they still stay beautiful.

F lowers come in all different sizes - tall, small,
L ovely they are with their delicate petals.
O pening their eyes,
W ith big smiles on their faces,
E njoying watching the flowers open,
R ich variety of stunning styles.

Megan Armitstead (10)
Beecroft Primary School

Smiling And Sadness

Smiling
S miling to someone who is upset
M ake someone smile, even the teachers
I make other people smile, why don't you?
L et's cheer somebody up
I smile every day, so smile, OK?
N ever feel down if somebody's words get you down
G ive someone a chin up, OK?

Sadness
S adness is not a good thing
A smile should cheer someone who is feeling down
D ays go on and on
N ever feel down
E veryone smiling
S ay to someone, 'Smile,' even if they're feeling down
S ay for the last time, *'Smile!'*

Mikayla Linley (10)
Beecroft Primary School

Winter Trees

W ild and wiry,
I ndividual leaves scattered on the ground,
N ot a single leaf on a tree,
T all, tender trunk,
E verlasting roots that dig deep underground,
R idged twigs that twist like a lost maze.

T owering hundreds of feet high,
R eaching out with its elegant fingers,
E njoying the whistling wind,
E vil, stretching twigs,
S hivering silently whilst crying winter's pain.

Alexandra Mardell (10)
Beecroft Primary School

Giant Winter

Giant Winter steals the Earth from the autumn.
Gripping the Earth with his icicle claws,
He squeezes away all colours,
Nothing can stop me.

Giant Winter turns the trees to skeletons,
Draining the Earth like a sponge.
Seeds snuggling down into the warm,
Soil hoping they don't die.

Giant Winter sneers at them as they struggle,
Sending a terrible frost.
Little deer charge through the forest,
He feels confident that he will take charge of the Earth.

Giant Winter feels like he is wining,
Suddenly he is getting smaller.
He hears a small, gentle laugh,
Giant Spring has arrived and saved the Earth once more.

Kimberley Allinson (10)
Beecroft Primary School

If The World Was Perfect

If the world was perfect,
Wars would end,
Broken bones would amend,
There would be no more dirty looks,
But everyone reading poetry books,
Friends would be there,
Countries would share,
And there would be no such thing as nightmares,
If the world was perfect,
There would be peace.

Emma Varley (11)
Beecroft Primary School

Eagle Glides

E agle flies above the horizon,
A nd tears into the unexpected victim,
G allant and bold,
L anding smoothly on the ground,
E agle flies away and looks at his nearest prey.

G igantic wings move gracefully through the evening sky,
L avishingly gliding amongst the treetops,
I nvading the prey's body,
D isrespecting the environment,
E vil eyes look through the prey,
S ilently, swiftly he swoops away.

Shyam Chohan (11)
Beecroft Primary School

Rainbow

R ain, rain go away, come back another day
A rainbow is multicoloured
I know what makes a rainbow
N ever go and see if you can get the gold
B ow is from a little boy in the woods
O h yes, a rainbow
W hat do you like about rainbows?

Gemma Blair (10)
Beecroft Primary School

Can You Name It?

What would you call this animal?
He's proud, he prowls and he roars,
He's stronger than anyone else,
His coat is the colour of straw.

Shelley Horne (9)
Beecroft Primary School

The Sea Horse

The sea horse is . . .
A small, colourful, timid fish
That swims in the gigantic turquoise ocean.
She regains her strength
And anchors herself up to a hideaway
From the writhing corals
And the swishing, threatening, deep blue waves
Slapping against the sandy rocks.
As she straightens up her tail and rises
Closer to the ripples on top,
She then hunts down her prey
That hides away beneath the sand.
Her eye stares at you in both directions,
So beware, she might be looking at you,
Any time you're down in her lair!

Sarah Larner (10)
Beecroft Primary School

Owl

Owl
Eyes of amber,
Gleam.
Feathers soft and ruffled,
Flap.
Talons of steel,
Clamp.
Jagged beak,
Tears.

Owl
Gulps
And screeches.
Owl swoops silently away
Through the silence
Of night.

Hugo Haggerty (10)
Beecroft Primary School

Tyrannosaurus Rex

The Tyrannosaurus rex is . . .
A reckless brute scouring the landscape
Searching for its petrified prey
Killing and eating every kind of herbivore
He finds a pack of Dienonychus drinking from his rippling river
Using his brute force he fends off the intruders
Mates with a female and wanders off
Then dying of old age the cumbersome titan falls into eternal sleep
For us to find his hollow skeleton in the next millennium.

Joseph Wren (10)
Beecroft Primary School

The Powerful Owl

Owl
Powerful as the eagle,
That dominates silently with fear.
Soon he would furiously come out as white as snow.

Beauty covered his power,
As he clamps his talons,
Like the forceps of a surgeon.

He is indeed an eagle in disguise.

Baha Tashani (11)
Beecroft Primary School

Flowers

Flowers are as sweet as sweets.
Flowers are as colourful as a rainbow.
Flowers are as delicate as butterflies.
Flowers are as bright as the sun.
Flowers are as silky as a ribbon.

Emily Charles (9)
Beecroft Primary School

The Adventures Of Isabel

Isabel met a powerful magician
Isabel was in good condition
The magician was nuts, the magician was crazy
He had a wand that fired a laser
'Ha, ha, ha, you cannot defeat me,' the magician roared
'I am too powerful for your tiny sword'
Isabel, Isabel didn't worry
Isabel didn't scream or scurry
She drew her sword and stabbed him hard
And the magician vanished and landed on Mars.

Aleem Islam (9)
Blenheim Primary School

My Mum

My mum is kind to all my family
My mum is like a burning fire which can never die out
My mum is brilliant

My mum helps me when I have cuts and bruises
My mum is like a hot, sunny beach which always stays sunny
My mum is totally the best

My mum cooks me my dinner
My mum is like a daffodil in spring which can never die
My mum is the best mum in the whole wide world.

Adam Flynn (9)
Blenheim Primary School

What Is A . . . Parrot?

He is a multicoloured tree.
It is a beautiful beach.
It is a smooth table.
It is a frightened snail.

Sohaib Hussain (9)
Blenheim Primary School

The Adventures Of Isabel

Isabel met a scary monster
Isabel carried on eating her lobster
The monster was big, the monster was scary
He had a red beard and was extremely hairy
'Isabel,' the monster screamed
'I'll eat you for dinner with chicken and cream,'
Isabel, Isabel didn't scream or scurry
She took her knife and chopped his hand
And ate him for breakfast with some bread!

Faraaz Waka (9)
Blenheim Primary School

Weather

The blaze of the sun is fire of the dragon
The noise of the thunder is the giants moving their chairs and tables
The howl is the howl of the wolves
The rain is the angels spitting down below
The light is the love of everyone
The dark is everyone's badness
The shade is the wings of a giant eagle.

Oliver Barry (9)
Blenheim Primary School

What Is . . . A Lion?

A lion is a very scary animal.
A lion is a hairy ball with red eyes.
A lion is a bad dream.
A lion is a brown animal.
A lion has fangs and they are very scary.
A lion has a very big mouth.

Abdihamed Ahmed (10)
Blenheim Primary School

What Is . . . A Cloud?

A cloud is a fluffy white ball of wool
floating in the summer's sky.

A cloud is a grey hot air balloon
flying high in the sky.

A cloud is a soft, white blanket
covering the grey sky.

A cloud is an imaginary shape
on a bright blue duvet.

A cloud is a grey piece of paper
floating on top of the playground.

A cloud is a roll of candyfloss
flying in the sky.

Danyang Li (10)
Blenheim Primary School

What Is . . . The Moon?

The moon is a piece of cheese
on a dark plate.

It is a great white shark
swimming in the sea.

It is a light bulb
hanging on the ceiling.

It is a silver button
sewed on a black shirt.

It is a five pence coin
lying alone in the empty streets.

Star Tong (10)
Blenheim Primary School

Mum!

'Mum, please help me do my homework?'
'In a minute Daughter.'
'But I'll get in trouble with my teacher.'
'When I've got some water.'

'Mum! There's a cobra under the table!'
'In a minute Daughter.'
'It has yellow teeth and it has a big tongue.'
'When I've got some water.'

'Mum! Its coming forwards!'
'In a minute Daughter.'
'But it's coming up the table and it's eating my breakfast.'
'When I've got some water.'

'Daughter, there's a cobra on the table.'
'In a minute Mum.'
'It's coming to get me. *Help me! Help!*'
'When I've got this done.'

Fatema Zaghloul (9)
Blenheim Primary School

What Is . . . A Ghost?

A ghost is a white gust of wind
Even blows out a candle in the dark

It is an invisible white figure
That can walk through walls coming from above

It is a white sheet of paper
Floating in the air

It is a haunting out of a bad dream
That is not going home

It is a figure from another world
That comes down to Earth.

Thomas Wade (10)
Blenheim Primary School

The Adventures Of Isabel

Isabel met a giant dragon
Isabel thumped it with a wagon
The dragon was powerful, the dragon was scary
It had a sword and a shield plus an evil fairy
'Isabel,' the dragon screamed
'I bet you wish you were in a dream?'
Isabel, Isabel didn't worry
Isabel didn't scream or scurry
She stole his sword and cut his head off
She took his wings and was off like a moth.

Bradley Holmes (9)
Blenheim Primary School

The Adventures Of Isabel

Isabel met a horrible dinosaur
Isabel heard his thunderous roar
The dinosaur was fat, its stomach was big
It had two heads, a right and a left
'Oooh Isabel,' the dinosaur screamed
Isabel, Isabel didn't worry
Isabel didn't scream or scurry
She said, 'Ooh dinosaur you have a nasty surprise'
And cut the dinosaur down to size.

Simone Dunshime (9)
Blenheim Primary School

What Is . . . A Kitten?

A kitten is a fluffy ball of fur with four legs,
A little pink nose and little green eyes.
A kitten is a white bundle of fur.
It is soft, fluffy and very playful.
It is snugly and cuddly.
Care for your kitten and you will be happy!

Layla Al-Muhtaseb (9)
Blenheim Primary School

What Is . . . Australia?

Australia is a hot bush in the sun,
It is a rocky mountain reaching high,
It is a coyote hot and bothered,
Australia is a ball floating in the sea,
It is a hot sun formed like an island,
Australia is a dry mouth waiting for water,
It is a desert baking in the sun,
Australia is a floating desert on the sea,
It is a koala bear slowly moving around.

Michael Fisher (9)
Blenheim Primary School

What Is . . . My Mum?

She is a warm blanket wrapped around me
She is a beautiful woman
She makes me safe when something bad happens
She has black hair and green eyes
She is someone who cares for me
She is the best mum in the world
She is soft and cool
She is my bed pillow, so cuddly.

Kyle Stewart (10)
Blenheim Primary School

Animals

A nimals are friendly, some are wild, some are smart
N octurnal animals come out at night
 I magine animals playing out
M ammals are large, mammals are tiny
A nimals are amazing creatures
L ullabies might put them to sleep
S o that's why I love *animals!*

Mark Adalat-Walker (9)
Blenheim Primary School

The Witch's Spell

Double, double, toil and trouble,
Fire burn and cauldron bubble.
Stomach of a hungry rat,
In the cauldron shout and chat.
Eye of newt and intestine of slug,
Sure he is just a little bug.
Human lungs and brain of bat,
Adder's heart and hippo's fat.
To make a slime paste of great trouble,
And in the cauldron it boils and bubbles.
Double, double, toil and trouble,
Fire burn and cauldron bubble.

Bobby Xu (10)
Blenheim Primary School

The Witches' Spell!

Double, double, toil and trouble,
Fire burn and cauldron bubble.
Vampire fangs and toe of frog,
A mouse's tail that's stuck in a log.
In the cauldron tail of slug,
Eye of newt and electric plug.
Fly's wing and a bee's sting,
Dinosaur's eye, parrot's wing.
For some gruesome trouble,
Make the cauldron bubble and bubble.
Double, double, toil and trouble,
Fire burn and cauldron bubble.

Raheem Johanneson (10)
Blenheim Primary School

The Witch's Spell

Double, double, toil and trouble,
Fire burn and cauldron bubble.
Fillet of a poisonous adder,
In the cauldron with a bladder.
Eye of a newt and ear of cat,
Leg of a frog and wing of a bat.
Beak of a bird, an eye of a spider,
Sting of a bee, mixed with cider.
A disgusting mixture for powerful trouble,
Everything in it will make it bubble.
Double, double, toil and trouble,
Fire burn and cauldron bubble.

Judy Li (10)
Blenheim Primary School

The Adventures Of Isabel

Isabel met a scary stallion
Isabel carried on feeding her lion
The stallion was big, the stallion was keen
It had a long neck, it was cruel and mean
The stallion said, 'Isabel, what are you doing?
I'd like to eat you,' he said cooing
Isabel, Isabel didn't worry
Isabel didn't scream or scurry
She caught him quick and threw a brick
And then she made the stallion sick.

Sherelle Dearing (10)
Blenheim Primary School

The Haunted Hospital

At ward fourteen
of this ultra modern
hospital

in the dead
middle
of the night

the little boy
wakes up
suddenly.

The little boy
hears moaning
and talking.

In the dead
middle
of the night

he sees a light
flickering
at the end of the ward

and sees a figure
with a gun
standing there.

All alone
in his bed
in the middle of the night.

Suddenly
the figure
disappears.

Clutching his teddy
he follows
the mystery figure

into ward thirteen
where men lie
bleeding on their beds

talking of the war
and tragedies
that have come upon them.

Not wanting to disturb
them
he quickly scurries
back to bed.

Next morning
at sunrise
the boy goes back.

In this ultra modern
hospital
there is no ward thirteen.

Jaye Rumney (10)
Christ Church Upper Armley CE Primary School

A Cat

Mouse catcher
Sofa scratcher
Heater sleeper
Crying weeper
Miaowing machine
Ripping a magazine
Looking for a key
Sipping down for some tea
His mother awakes and goes to get some cakes
Who am I?

Ambriya Iqbal (9)
Christ Church Upper Armley CE Primary School

The Haunted Hospital

At ward fourteen
of this ultra modern
hospital

in the dead
middle
of the night

a boy wakes up
to a painful
crying sound.

He follows the
painful sound
to ward thirteen.

In the dead
middle
of the night

the lights are
flickering
on and off.

In the distance
he can hear voices
like soldiers.

He runs back
to his bed and
tries to sleep.

In the morning
he wakes up.
Was it a dream?

He tiptoes
back to
ward thirteen.

At this ultra modern hospital
there is no ward
thirteen.

Kirsty Warren (10)
Christ Church Upper Armley CE Primary School

Footsteps

Tip, tap,
Tip, tap,
Footsteps echo through the night,
Shivers running down my spine.
Tip, tap,
Tip, tap,
The footsteps coming up the stairs,
I shut my window and lock my door.
Tip, tap,
Tip, tap,
My brother is fast asleep,
I'm all alone tortured by my fears.
Tip, tap,
Tip, tap,
My door creaks slightly, someone's there!
Then as I hold my breath the door swings open.
Tip, tap,
Tip, tap,
A ghostly girl is standing there,
But I no longer fear her.
Tip, tap,
Tip, tap,
She looks as scared as I am!
I stretch out my hand and touch her arm.
Tip, tap,
Tip, tap,
The girl retreats, I hear a sigh,
'Until tomorrow!' whispers the night.
Tip, tap,
Tip, tap.

Emily Owen (11)
Christ Church Upper Armley CE Primary School

The Wanahogalooga

It was a few years ago
a man-eating monster
was born.

Beware of the evil Wanahogalooga,
it will eat your flesh, bones
and everything.

It is said that it lives
behind the tallest mountain,
under the deepest cave
and through the darkest forests.

'My dear daughter
beware of your journey,
the Wanahogalooga is dangerous,
he'll eat you, destroy you!'

So she went on her journey,
looking through the mountain,
through the underground caves,
and the darkest forests.

Through and through
the sword attacks,
the mighty Wanahogalooga will fall.
He, the Wanahogalooga
is *dead!*

Emylie Periot-McCann (11)
Christ Church Upper Armley CE Primary School

Giggling Geography

Australia's angry
Bahrain's bossy
Cuba's cube-shaped
Delta's going dotty
Estonia's done an eggie
France loves fish
Georgia's gorgeous
Hungary's hungry
Iran's incredible
Jordan's jelly
Korea's kingfisher
Libya's little
Madagascar's mischievous
Nigeria's nibbling
Oman's odd
Philippine's party
Qatar's question
Russia's rude
Saudi Arabia's silly
Turkey loves turkey
USA's ugly
Vatican city's vicious
Wales is wobbly
X is nothing
Yugoslavia's yoghurt
Zambia's a zombie.

Michael Bonallie (9)
Christ Church Upper Armley CE Primary School

The Summer Environment

The trees they stood
In the summer wood
They will not see me passing through
But only if I knew
I'd make them greener if I could

The green summer grass
Swaying as I pass
Departing a path for me
As far as I could see
And walking as if to trespass

The sweet smell of flowers I can smell
So lovely and pleasant filling me with dwell
The colour of flowers just like a long rainbow
Like red, orange, blue and yellow
I feel like a wonderful snail in a warm shell

The winter's coming, no green will show
The trees, the flowers, all these lovely things will go
I'll wait by this tree until summer comes around
This is the place I'll stand till summer is found.

Saida Lodhi (10)
Christ Church Upper Armley CE Primary School

Brother For Sale!

Christopher Adam Hardisty, born in 1996, age 7 years old.
He is interested in basketball and football.
He throws tantrums if he is with a girl.
Doesn't like reading, doesn't like homework.
Only apply if you are aged 6-8 years old!
I will exchange for a large sum of money.

Katie Louise Hardisty (10)
Christ Church Upper Armley CE Primary School

Cats, Cats, Cats

Big cats, small cats
More cats, more cats
Black cats, brown cats
Very, very tall cats
I love cats!

Sleeping cats, playing cats
More cats, more cats
Hungry cats, fat cats
Cats, cats, cats
I love cats!

Grey cats, white cats
More cats, more cats
Fluffy cats, friendly cats
Vicious cats, cute cats
Cuddly cats

We need more cats
Frisky cats, bad cats
Crazy cats, new cats
Old cats, young cats
Skinny cats, stray cats
I love cats!

Purring cats, scaredy cats
Brainy cats, kitty cats
More cats, more cats
Silly cats, diva cats
Tom cats, lazy cats
Purrrrrfect!

Siobhan Sprakes (10)
Christ Church Upper Armley CE Primary School

Training Day!

Mum: 'Come on Fred.'
Fred: I heave out of bed.
Mum: 'Brush your teeth.'
Fred: 'OK, OK, don't give me grief.'
Mum: 'Wash your face and hurry up!'
Fred: I swill my mouth out with my cup.
Mum: 'Come on Fred or you'll be late.'
Fred: 'OK, OK, it's only eight.'
Mum: 'Get dressed and come down here right now!'
Fred: I'll get her with my gun, *pow!*
Mum: 'Come and get your breakfast.'
Fred: 'OK Mum, I'm down at last.'
Mum: 'Come on then and get your bag.'
Fred: 'It's only 8.30, don't nag!'
Mum: 'Hooray, we're at school at last.'
Fred: 'But it's a training day, oh blast!'

Alice Rowland (10)
Christ Church Upper Armley CE Primary School

Who Am I? - Kennings

I am a . . .
tree climber
tail winder

loud scream
cheeky not mean

banana keeper
good leaper

ooh, argh squeaker
climbing steeper

Tarzan friend
flexible end

Who am I?
A: I am a monkey!

Dani Rice (10)
Christ Church Upper Armley CE Primary School

Strange Noises

Can you hear the noises?
I think there's something there
There's always something creaking
At the bottom of the stairs!

Run into your bedroom
And lock the door tight
Because something supernatural
Is coming round tonight!

Go under your covers
Pretend you are asleep
For the creature is coming near now
In your bedroom it will creep!

The morning draws nearer
The creature will go away
But tomorrow it will come again
Tomorrow is another day!

Charlotte Clough (10)
Christ Church Upper Armley CE Primary School

The Grim Reaper

The moon shines on the shed
And I have just got to my bed
I hear the rustling from the shed
It comes into my house and up the stairs
I lock my door and shut the window.

I hear a knife cutting through my brother's door
My heart stops, I cannot breathe
The Grim Reaper will not leave
My brother must have been on his list to slay
He must have known it was my brother's last day.

Adeel Qayum (10)
Christ Church Upper Armley CE Primary School

Spring

The seasons have come to spring,
What brightness could it bring?
It will be bright,
In the middle of the night,
You will hear the songbirds sing.

Jennifer Midgley (9)
Christ Church Upper Armley CE Primary School

Cauldron Bubble

Bubble, bubble, double trouble,
In the fizzy cauldron,
Snake skins in,
Pop in the bin,
While the cauldron bubbles.

Bubble, bubble, double trouble,
In the whizzing cauldron,
Bats' wings in,
Pop in the bin,
While the cauldron fizzes.

Bubble, bubble, double trouble,
In the sparkling cauldron,
Frogs' legs in,
Pop in the bin,
While the cauldron whizzes.

That's how you make a spell.

Javehn Taylor (9)
Cobden Primary School

Olympic Games

Loads of smelly feet
Oh what a treat!
Who will win?
Who will break a shin?

A swimmer is a fast train
A weightlifter is a crane
A sprinter is a rabbit low
A pole vaulter is a good show.

A wrestler is an unbreakable truck
A gymnastic is a flying duck
A long jumper is a super man
A rower is a strong man.

Jake Grundy (8)
Cobden Primary School

Special Friends

Special friends are people you can trust,
Who are always there to listen,
And are always on a mission,
When watching television.

They will come and play,
Any day in May,
Even on a rainy day,
To stay out of the way.

When you feel sad,
Your friends will go mad,
But it makes you feel glad,
Special friends like you are fab.

Claire Bland (9)
Cobden Primary School

My Football Match

My football match was really fun,
I went to score a goal,
Instead I slipped and hurt my bum,
And then I fell down a hole.

The referee stopped the game,
And rushed to my assistance,
He picked me up and brushed me down,
So I could do the distance.

I kicked the ball into the net,
The crowd were screaming wildly,
It moved as fast as a jumbo jet,
My face was beaming proudly.

Bradley Wilson (10)
Cobden Primary School

Horse

Swish, swish, clatter, clatter
Gallop, gallop, na, na
As the horse trots by
Brush, brush, clip, clop
As you get washed

Canter, canter, panta, panta
Trot, trot, win, win
As you win a race
Swish, swish, clatter, clatter
Gallop, gallop, na, na
As the horse trots by.

Ellie Herridge
Cobden Primary School

Bogey Toby

B ogey Toby is always picking his nose,
O n his bed he wipes his bogies on his toes,
G one midnight he has a finger up his nose,
E verywhere he goes,
Y ou'll see him with a finger up his nose.

T he doctors don't dare cut off his fingers,
O n the stage he makes a terrible singer,
B ut at home he makes a horrible minger,
Y ou'll be sure to *pick* him for a contest.

Bryan Fenton (9)
Cobden Primary School

Mojo Hobo

M ojo is a hobo,
O n a street he sleeps,
J oe the monkey is his only friend,
O ut in the cold he sleeps.

H ated he is,
O n every street,
B ut he doesn't care,
O nly when he's bare.

Cainan McEwan (10)
Cobden Primary School

Family Poem

F is for family which are there for you always,
A is for apple which is not as sweet as you,
M is for month which I was born in,
I is for information that you gave me,
L is for love which you give me every day,
Y is for you which I love very much.

Robyn Middleton (9)
Cobden Primary School

Granny Rap!

(Based on 'Gran Can You Rap?' by Jack Ouseby)

Does your granny rap? Does your granny rap?
Does she wear a cap? Does she wear a cap?
Does she shout 'Yo, yo, yo, yo, kill the beat?'
Does she shout 'Yo, yo, yo, yo, kill the beat?'
Does she dance and kick her feet?
Does she dance and kick her feet?

Does your granny rap? Does your granny rap?
Does she make you tap? Does your granny make you tap?
Is your granny cool? Is your granny cool?
Does your granny rap when you're at school?
Does your granny rap when you're at school?

Does your granny rap? Does your granny rap?
Does she make your cat rap through the flap?
Does she make your cat rap through the flap?
Does your granny have a nap?
Does your granny have a nap?
Never, never, never, 'cause she's too into *rap!*

PS: Does your granny really *rap?*

Christopher Boyd (10)
Cobden Primary School

When I Go To School

I go to school each morning,
When I can't stop yawning.
In my lessons I'm wide awake,
Before I know it, it's time for morning break.

And then I'm home for dinner,
And I have a quick snack.
Before I know it,
I'm going back.

Kane Hirst (10)
Cobden Primary School

Lady Of Shalott

(Based on 'The Lady of Shalott' by Alfred Lord Tennyson)

What could the curse be?
When will it come upon me?
Who will save the lady?
She will be saved I hope,
I look at Camelot,
The tower's falling, one plant to catch,
It's a small, green plant,
The river's current is hard,
I will miss Shalott.

The glass is nearly gone,
It has shone,
Camelot jumps in, she cannot die,
He can see the clouds in the sky,
I can go back to Camelot,
Everyone has gone,
No one can have any fun,
And no one has won,
Bye-bye Camelot.

Samantha Joyce (8)
Cobden Primary School

About Friends

Friends are people who you need,
And if you're nice you will succeed.
Friends will help,
But if they're not nasty you won't yelp.
Friends give you a helping hand,
And play with you in the sand.
So that's what friends are for.

Holly Bannister (8)
Cobden Primary School

Holli No Friends

I sat alone and watched the world go by
I asked myself, 'Why, oh why?'
I then thought I would look up to the sky
And then to my surprise
The angels came to say, 'Hi there Holli, hi.'

We sat and listened and to my surprise
The pennies appeared to fall from the sky
I clapped and sung and danced around
To find there was no one else around.

I sat and pondered on my own
Now there is no one to call my own
Holli has no friends
And I am on my own

Then I awake only to find
Mummy and Daddy stood behind.

Holli Rutter **(9)**
Cobden Primary School

Playtimes

On a playtime we play games,
We run around with canes,
Sometimes we play football,
Sometimes we play basketball,
And we play cricket,
I always hit the wicket,
And when I bat I always hit it,
When I am fielder I always catch it,
Playtimes are always a big hit.

Ryan Gillen **(9)**
Cobden Primary School

My Friends

What I like about my friends
is when they always cheer you up, no matter what.
What I hate about my friends
is when they fall out with you over nothing.
What I like about my friends
is when you can always count on them to help you.
What I hate about my friends
is when they go off with another friend and only come back
when no one else is there.
What I like about my friends
is when you forget something and your friend lends you one of theirs.
What I hate about my friends
is when you have a sleepover and they don't stop talking.
What I like about my friends
is when you can tell secrets to them and know that they won't
tell a soul.

Annie Smith (11)
Gildersome Primary School

My Brothers

What I hate about my brothers is when they are mean
and gang up on me.
What I like about my brothers is when they are kind and nice to me.
What I hate about my brothers is when they hurt me
and say they didn't.
What I like about my brothers is when we play together.
What I hate about my brothers is when they take over the TV.
What I like about my brothers is when we help one another.
What I hate about my brothers is when they blame me for something
I didn't do.
What I like about my brothers is when we act like brothers
and care for each other.

Matthew Cross (10)
Gildersome Primary School

My Dad

What I hate about my dad
is when he shouts at me
for no reason at all.

> What I like about my dad
> is when he takes me on holiday
> to a sunny place.

What I hate about my dad
is when he doesn't
let me watch TV.

> What I like about my dad
> is when he orders films on the TV
> and he lets me stay up late.

What I hate about my dad
is he smokes
and it's not good for you.

> What I like about my dad
> is I feel safe
> when my dad is around.

James Stratton (11)
Gildersome Primary School

My Grandma

What I love about my grandma
is when I sit on her knee and she cuddles me.
  What I hate about my grandma
  is when I don't see her for days and days.
What I love about my grandma
is when she tickles my toes when I sit on her couch.
  What I hate about my grandma
  is when she goes on holiday and makes me jealous.
What I love about my grandma
is her cosy, hot chocolate that warms me up inside.
  What I hate about my grandma
  is when she makes me finish my tea even when I'm full.
What I love about my grandma
is when I'm poorly and she looks after me
even when I'm sick in her bed.
  What I hate about my grandma
  is when she is poorly and I can't look after her.
What I love about my grandma
is that she is always there by my side.

Jenny Bedford (10)
Gildersome Primary School

My Dad

What I like about my dad
is the warm welcome he gives me.

What I hate about my dad
is when he has to go to Cyprus for his work.

What I like about my dad
is when he sweet-talks my mum for me.

What I hate about my dad
is when he turns over to football.

What I like about my dad
is when he makes me laugh.

What I hate about my dad
is when he falls asleep
halfway through my singing concert.

Chloe Proctor (10)
Gildersome Primary School

My Dog

What I liked about my dog was that she was so cute and cuddly.
What I hated about my dog was when she was poorly
and she wouldn't play with me.
What I liked about my dog was that even though she was sixteen
she was still playful.
What I hated about my dog was when she used to squeak her toys
while I was watching TV.
What I liked about my dog was when she used to smile at me
but really she was just panting.
What I hated about my dog was when she'd been out in the rain
and I stroked her and she was wet.
What I liked about my dog was that she always gave me
a loving greeting on a morning.

Stephanie Waddle (11)
Gildersome Primary School

Summer

What I like about summer
Is when I can eat lots of ice creams.
What I hate about summer
Is when we run out of ice cream
And my mum forgets to buy more.

What I like about summer
Is when Annie and I go to the fields at the top of my street
And play all day.
What I hate about summer
Is when wasps and bees come over and give me a sting.

What I like about summer
Is when I go to my grandma's and I see my pen pal.
What I hate about summer
Is when I try to go to sleep but my covers stick to me.

What I like about summer
Is when I wake up and I have breakfast outside.

Abigail Webb (10)
Gildersome Primary School

Summer Holidays

What I hate about holidays is unpacking my case
and trying to find somewhere to put my clothes.
What I like about holidays is packing my case full of games to play.
What I hate about holidays is eating the awful food on the plane.
What I like about holidays is flying on the plane
and eating loads of sweets.
What I hate about holidays is going for really boring walks
to the middle of nowhere.
What I like about holidays is swimming in the pool or Jacuzzi.
What I hate about holidays is when my dad's drunk
and embarrasses me.
What I like about holidays is going to the beach
and getting hit by the waves.

Charlotte Smith (10)
Gildersome Primary School

My Grandad

What I hate about my grandad is
he never comes with us when my grandma takes us out.
What I like about my grandad is
he's always cheerful and smiley.

What I hate about my grandad is
when he's ill he can't come to my house.
What I like about my grandad is
when I'm coming he buys food he knows I like.

What I hate about my grandad is
he lives too far away!
What I like about my grandad is
he will take us absolutely anywhere.

What I hate about my grandad is
when we go to my cousin's he stays at home all alone.
What I like about my grandad is
when he tucks me up warm and cuddly.

Kirsten Parry (10)
Gildersome Primary School

My Cat

What I hate about my cat is when
she comes in my room in the middle of the night and miaows at me.
What I like about my cat is when
she wants to sit on my knee and she wants me to stroke her.
What I hate about my cat is when
she is laying on my comfy bed all day and leaves her hair on it.
What I like about my cat is when
she always cheers me up with her different colours
and makes me happy.
What I hate about my cat is when
she wants me to feed her but I am far too tired.
What I like about my cat is that
she always waits for me to come home.

Sophie Morton (10)
Gildersome Primary School

My Budgie

What I hate about my budgie
is when I'm watching the TV
it's very noisy.
    What I like about my budgie
    is that it's funny when I hear a bang
    because it's just fallen from its perch.
What I hate about my budgie
is when it chirps through the night
and I can't get to sleep.
    What I like about my budgie
    is that it's lovely and soft
    when I play with it.
What I hate about my budgie
is when it bites me
it feels like somebody's nipping you.
    What I like about my budgie
    is that it's cheerful, no matter what.

Jessica Hill (11)
Gildersome Primary School

The Magic Box

(Based on 'Magic Box' by Kit Wright)

I will put in the box . . .
The heat of a breathing dragon
The smell of roses and daffodils
The beautiful sea

I will put in the box . . .
A touch of a baby's hand
A picture of the seaside
Butterflies fluttering

I will put in the box . . .
The feel of a snowdrop on my nose
The smile of a baby
The glittering stars in the sky.

Amy Swales (7)
Hawksworth CE Primary School

The Magic Box

(Based on 'Magic Box' by Kit Wright)

I will put in the box . . .
The first word of a baby boy
The sweet scent of a rose
The excitement on Christmas Day

I will put in the box . . .
The first bark of a puppy
The soft feel of my teddy
The laughter of my baby cousin

I will put in the box . . .
A magic white unicorn and fly up in the sky
The beautiful colours of a rainbow
The fluttering sound of fairy wings

I will put in the box . . .
The feel of summer sun on my skin
The first bleating baby lamb in spring
The first snowflake on a winter's day

My box is made of many colours
It is lined with fairy dust and is hinged with golden thread
The key is made of golden jewels and silver gems

I will sit upon my box and float across a blue lagoon
Have fairy cakes with the fairy queen and fly upon a cloud
And dance and dance all day and night
Then I will sleep in my box.

Kristy Fawcett (9)
Hawksworth CE Primary School

The Magic Box

(Based on 'Magic Box' by Kit Wright)

I will put in the box . . .
The last words of my grandad
The fiery flames of a Welsh dragon
The glances of my mum and dad

I will put in the box . . .
A fat, flying pig
A house full of mountains
A mouse making friends with an elephant

I will put in the box . . .
The first friend I made
The first medal I won
The first goal I scored

I will put in the box . . .
A shark that could swim to the moon
An alien with a wooden leg
And a pirate with three eyes

My box is made of silver and wood
With the moon on the lid
And special thoughts on the edges
The hinges are kneecaps belonging to giraffes

I shall fly on my box through the star-filled sky
And rest on the clouds made of cotton wool.

Toby Mountain (9)
Hawksworth CE Primary School

The Magic Box

(Based on 'Magic Box' by Kit Wright)

I will put in the box . . .
A lick from a husky's tongue
The crunch of crispy autumn leaves
The flip flap of angels' wings

I will put in the box . . .
The colour blue
The smell of fresh air in Scotland
The taste of nice fresh oranges in the summer

I will put in the box . . .
A kiss from Mummy at bedtime
A hug from Daddy
The yawn from Bagpuss my alarm clock

I will put in the box . . .
The smell of birthday cake
The sound of ripping paper
The tingling bells of Santa's sleigh

My box is made from silver leather
With a bright red ruby
And a small gold lock and key

I would go to sleep on my box and have wonderful dreams
My dreams would be about dancing with my friends.

Amy Turk (8)
Hawksworth CE Primary School

The Magic Box

(Based on 'Magic Box' by Kit Wright)

I will put in the box . . .
The yellow flash of lightning,
The sound of tooting trumpets,
And the colours from the rainbow.

I will put in the box . . .
The beginning of the world,
A jelly fish's sting,
The gurgle of my guinea pig.

I will put in the box . . .
The twinkle of an eye,
Snow from the top of Mount Everest,
A falling leaf in autumn.

I will put in the box . . .
A shooting star,
A flying car,
A Christmas card from the moon.

My box is made of sweet dreams
And ribbons twisted together,
The key is a feather from the first peacock ever.
The box is lined with a universe.

I will stand on my box and fly through space,
And land on a planet made of toffee.

Elizabeth Heard (8)
Hawksworth CE Primary School

The Magic Box

(Based on 'Magic Box' by Kit Wright)

I will put in the box . . .
The sound of rushing water
The cheeping of newborn chicks
And the shining of the sun

I will put in the box . . .
The twinkling of the stars
A halo from an angel
And the memories of Christmas Day

I will put in the box . . .
Money of different countries
The taste of Cornish pasties
And the dreams out of a dreamcatcher.

Charlotte Fisher (8)
Hawksworth CE Primary School

The Magic Box

(Based on 'Magic Box' by Kit Wright)

I will put in the box . . .
A dinosaur
A piece of silver
A golden ring

I will put in the box . . .
A walking clock
A snowman with everlasting snow
A lamp that will never go out

I will put in the box . . .
A candle that will never go out
A key that was made out of diamond
An everlasting movie.

Ben Swinton (8)
Hawksworth CE Primary School

The Magic Box

(Based on 'Magic Box' by Kit Wright)

I will put in the box . . .
The last breath of my mother
The first tear from a baby
My first word

I will put in the box . . .
A whisker from my cat
The first kiss I ever had
The first flower I ever grew

I will put in the box . . .
My baby's first curl
A crispy autumn leaf
My christening bracelet.

Ella Hainsworth-Brear (8)
Hawksworth CE Primary School

The Magic Box

(Based on 'Magic Box' by Kit Wright)

I will put in the box . . .
The last stroke of Jill my dog
The feel of my best teddy called Eddy

I will put in the box . . .
The memory of my auntie Kathleen's paperweight
And Jonny Wilkinson's boot

I will put in the box . . .
The smell of Boss aftershave
And the smell of shower gel.

Adam Laycock (8)
Hawksworth CE Primary School

The Magic Box

(Based on 'Magic Box' by Kit Wright)

I will put in the box . . .
A little mouse squeak
A flame of a warm lit fire
An everlasting bug

I will put in the box . . .
A silver biscuit
A crow that never caws
A one million pound cheque

I will put in the box . . .
A rose and a buttercup
An ice lolly that never melts
The brightest star in the sky

I will put in the box . . .
The sun and the moon
The very first light
A sparkly broach

I will put in the box . . .
A fluffy cloud
A puppy dog
A monkey swinging through the trees

I will put in the box . . .
The last berry
The first petal
A ray form the sun

I will put in the box . . .
A kitten
A hamster
And a Shetland pony.

Amy Hill (9)
Hawksworth CE Primary School

The Magic Box

(Based on 'Magic Box' by Kit Wright)

I will put in the box . . .
The first rose of spring
A kiss from your mum and dad
A first snowflake of winter

I will put in the box . . .
My first pet Benson
A first birthday with presents
My bestest friend Amy

I will put in the box . . .
My favourite teddy dog
My first smile
My family and TV

I will put in the box . . .
My best teacher, Mr R
My friend Richard
My fairy friends, the rainbow fairies.

Claire McFetridge (7)
Hawksworth CE Primary School

The Magic Box

(Based on 'Magic Box' by Kit Wright)

I will put in the box . . .
The first bark of a baby puppy
The first drop of a tree
The first cry of a baby

I will put in the box . . .
The smell of bread just been cooked
The smell of chocolate muffins in the oven
The smell of melted chocolate to make buns.

Olivia Armstrong (8)
Hawksworth CE Primary School

The Magic Box

(Based on 'Magic Box' by Kit Wright)

I will put in the box . . .
The first red sunset of summer,
The last dawn of spring,
The last unicorn's horn.

I will put in the box . . .
The last leaf of autumn,
The first noise of a cat,
The last pirate's hat.

I will put in the box . . .
The first gulp of a fish,
The last lit candle,
The first shark's tooth,
The smell of the Queen's perfume,
The sound of baby Jesus.

Sophie Whitham (9)
Hawksworth CE Primary School

The Magic Box

(Based on 'Magic Box' by Kit Wright)

I will put in the box . . .
The smell of bacon sandwiches
The taste of mushy peas
The taste of blackcurrant juice

I will put in the box . . .
The smell of fish and chips
The taste of chocolate chip cookies
The touch of wibbly wobbly jelly.

Bethany Williamson (7)
Hawksworth CE Primary School

The Magic Box

(Based on 'Magic Box' by Kit Wright)

In my box I will put . . .
The feel of fire that does not hurt
A crown made out of fish
Jewels in a swishing sea

In my box I will put . . .
One single drop of water
A tooth of a shark
A little crumb of pea

In my box I will put . . .
Every single blade of grass
My very best friends
A tooth from God

My box is made out of gold
With a mixture of pearls and rubies
It has legs of beautiful gold
Carved like delicate flower

I will ride on my box
And it will take me to the land of imagination
Where all my wishes will come true.

Emma Pickersgill (8)
Hawksworth CE Primary School

The Magic Box

(Based on 'Magic Box' by Kit Wright)

I will put into my box . . .
A smell of the open sea
Jesus' special star from the midnight sky
And all my family

I will put into my box . . .
A sparkly fish with jewels
A bird with twinkling wings
And all my friends.

Daniel Holt (8)
Hawksworth CE Primary School

The Magic Box
(Based on 'Magic Box' by Kit Wright)

I will put in the box . . .
A flying dog
A dinosaur
A piece of gold

I will put in the box . . .
A sword that is as big as the world
A walking pencil
A gold football

I will put in the box . . .
An everlasting sweet
A talking chair
An everlasting movie.

Adam Swinton (8)
Hawksworth CE Primary School

The Magic Box
(Based on 'Magic Box' by Kit Wright)

I will put in the box . . .
The taste of a fresh piece of bread
A mother's hug coming from the heart
The smell of a freshly baked apple pie

I will put in the box . . .
A shining star high up in the sky
A bright coloured sun
A seven-foot dinosaur

I will put in the box . . .
An apple on an aeroplane
A tortoise up a tree
A dog that's cradling a chick.

Sarah Tate (8)
Hawksworth CE Primary School

The Magic Box
(Based on 'Magic Box' by Kit Wright)

I will put in the box . . .
The longest piece of grass in the world
All the creature comforts
The Loch Ness monster

I will put in the box . . .
The colour of daffodils
The soft fur of a cat
The smell of chicken cooking

I will put in the box . . .
A chocolate cigar with coffee truffle in the middle
The last bit of white snow
The biggest fish that's ever been caught

My box is made out of chocolate cake and cream
And decorated with strawberries.

Louis Barker (7)
Hawksworth CE Primary School

The Magic Box
(Based on 'Magic Box' by Kit Wright)

I will put in the box . . .
The smell of sizzling bacon
The light of the silver moon
And the sight of a twinkling star.

I will put in the box . . .
The smell of Grandma's bread
My very best friend
My mummy's cuddle.

I will put in the box . . .
A picture of my great grandma
A piece of apple pie
And Rosie my rabbit.

Claudia Marchbank (7)
Hawksworth CE Primary School

The Magic Box

(Based on 'Magic Box' by Kit Wright)

I will put in the box . . .
11 dancing bears in swimming costumes
Snow from the North Pole
Ice cream melting in the cone

I will put in the box . . .
7 seas with a boat
100 trees with a bird
6 rings with a diamond

I will put in the box . . .
A Viking's sharp axe
A ruler to measure size
A vision of Heaven

I will put in the box . . .
A dog with a mouse
A cat with a bone
A book with moving pictures

My box is gold on top
With silver hinges
Supported by mice's feet
With a pearl lock and key

I shall take my box to bed, school,
Bowling, church and everywhere.

Katharine Foxton (8)
Hawksworth CE Primary School

The Magic Box

(Based on 'Magic Box' by Kit Wright)

I will put in my box . . .
The memory of my grandma
The roar of my favourite dinosaur
Mummy's and Daddy's hugs

I will put in my box . . .
The snow we played in at New Year
Legolas from Lord of the Rings
My new book 'The Hobbit'

I will put in my box . . .
My first Manchester United football kit
My first goal scored
My first goal saved

I will put in my box . . .
A witch who can only do good spells
A three-headed red and blue monster

My box is made of all things nice
With bright coloured jewels all around
The hinges are made of gold and are the shape of my hands

I shall jog on my box for miles and miles around the world
And stop in Australia for a nap!

Joseph Mountain (7)
Hawksworth CE Primary School

It Was So Silent That I Heard . . .

It was so silent that I heard
Mrs Twit grumbling at the muggle-wumps.

It was so silent that I heard
The trees whooshing the leaves of the branches.

It was so silent that I heard
The owl going *'Ooooo!'* outside on the branch.

Temur Al-Jihad (8)
Hovingham Primary School

It Was So Silent

It was so silent that I heard
Leaves rustling in the tall trees.

It was so silent that I heard
A man walking outside.

It was so silent that I heard
Wind blowing the flowers and trees.

It was so silent that I heard
The clock ticking downstairs.

It was so silent that I heard
The floorboards creaking.

It was so silent that I heard
A pin drop.

Sahiba Sajid (7)
Hovingham Primary School

My Silent Poem

It was so silent that I heard
A little pin drop from the brown table.

It was so silent that I heard
A floorboard creak like an old leg.

It was so silent that I heard
A man whistling in the wind.

It was so silent that I heard
My mum talking outside in the garden.

It was so silent that I heard
An owl going, 'Tu-whit tu-whoo' in the darkness.

Max Lee (7)
Hovingham Primary School

A Poem To Be Spoken Silently

It was so silent that I heard
The clock saying, 'Tick-tock,' on top of the fire.

It was so silent that I heard
A lady tiptoeing next to the window.

It was so silent that I heard
The wind blowing through the chimney.

It was so silent that I heard
The leaves falling off the tree.

Alisha Liaqat (7)
Hovingham Primary School

It Was So Silent

It was so silent that I heard
The wind blowing the leaves from the trees.

It was so silent that I heard,
The drip as water was slipping down the window.

It was so silent that I heard
The floorboard creaking as the insect walked.

Mehreen Ali (8)
Hovingham Primary School

It Was So Silent That . . .

It was so silent that I heard
A bird singing on the top of the roof.

It was so silent that I heard
The clock ticking in the hall.

It was so silent that I heard
The wind blow the leaves off the trees.

Adnan Mohammed (8)
Hovingham Primary School

The Storm

The dustbin falls, crash, crash
The lightning goes, flash, flash
The thunder goes, dash, dash
The car headlights go, flash, flash.

In a scary, fierce night
A terrible wind came to fight.
It's too windy to fly a kite,
A terrible wind comes to fight.

The dustbin falls, crash, crash
The lightning goes, flash, flash
The thunder goes, dash, dash
The car headlights go, flash, flash.

Natasha Saeed (8)
Hovingham Primary School

My Silent Poem

It was so silent that I heard
A stranger whistle in the silent wind.

It was so silent that I heard
A curtain move in my house.

It was so silent that I heard
A swing rattle in the park.

It was so silent that I heard
A dog bark in my garden.

It was so silent that I heard
A flower springing in the sunshine.

Aamir Ali (7)
Hovingham Primary School

It Was So Silent That . . .

It was so silent that I heard
The mice squeaking in the dirty sewers.
It was so silent that I heard
A dog barking
From miles away.
It was so silent that I heard
The creepy and squeaky floorboards in the lounge.
It was so silent that I heard
The cans twirling and swirling in the street.
It was so silent that I heard
The rapping music at the midnight club.
It was so silent that I heard
The fire crackling downstairs.
It was so silent that I heard
The water dripping down from the tap.
It was so silent that I heard
The foxes getting all the chicken bones with flesh on from the bin.
It was so silent that I heard
The next-door neighbours snoring in their beds.

Jonathan Brown (8)
Hovingham Primary School

Acrostic Poem

T he Nile floods every summer
H eavy thick mud is left by the flood.
E very year people make bricks with the mud.

N ile is the gift of Egypt
I n Egypt people ride boats slowly on the Nile
L ots of people make things with the mud
E very year people are happy when there is a flood.

Moheen Khan (7)
Hovingham Primary School

The Noisy Poem

Rain falls splash, splash
Cameras click flash, flash
Windows crack clash, clash
Cars stop bash, bash.

In the busy wide street
Clippety, cloppety huge feet
People go running down the street
Clippety, cloppety huge feet.

Rain falls, splash, splash
Cameras click, flash, flash
Windows crack, clash, clash
Cars stop bash, bash.

A wedding comes to a big hall
The people are all big and tall
Go dashing into the big, big hall
The people all are big and tall.

Farhana Yasin (8)
Hovingham Primary School

Missing You

Although you may be far away
We still think of you every day
You're in our hearts
And in our minds
We'll always treasure those happy times
If you could be here
For just one day
So many things
We have to say
We miss you all so very much
So please, please, please get back in touch.

Ashleigh Myers (10)
Lawns Park Primary School

Family

When I'm at home
I'm never alone
I'm with my family and friends
And the fun never ends.

When my friends come round
We make one heck of a sound
My mum doesn't moan
Cos she's usually on the phone.

I've got a sister called Laura-May
She's sometimes known to snore away
She kicks all day
Never getting tired of play.

My nana lives not far from me
So plenty of her I do see.
My cousin Jake is usually there
He's a little boy with not much hair.

When the day ends
I say bye to my friends
Then we have our tea
Mum, Laura and me.

Nathaniel Harrison (9)
Lawns Park Primary School

Misty

A misty day,
A misty dawn.

A misty night,
A misty yawn.

A misty bird in the sky,
A misty star way up high.

A misty statue still as a steeple,
Looks around yet sees no people.

Amy Robinson (11)
Lawns Park Primary School

Kangaroo Emerged

Kangaroo emerged,
She stole the spring of a frog,
She stole the pounce of a lion,
And created her jump.

Then at night,
She stole the colour of the sand,
She stole the softness of the silk,
And made her coat.

From the large forests,
She stole the balance of a tree,
She stole the length of a puddle,
And made her tail.

For her pouch,
She stole the softness of a feather,
She stole the warmth of a fire,
She stole the comfort of an armchair.

For her feet,
She stole the beat of a drum,
She stole the size of a hare's feet,
She stole the weight of an elephant.

And Kangaroo was made.

Emma McVey (11)
Lawns Park Primary School

Plums

P is for pear as green as an apple
L   is for lightning zigzagging across the sky.
U is for umbrella to keep off the rain.
M is for my sweet mother.
S   is for sunshine which makes everyone happy.

Rebekka Danby (9)
Lawns Park Primary School

My Friends

I have a friend called Josh,
Who thinks he's really posh.
His favourite food is cheese,
He's a real funny disease.

I have a friend called Jamie,
Who has a crush on Amy.
He always wants to play,
And he likes to have a say.

I have a friend called Ben,
Whose favourite mate is Ken.
His best hobby is sport,
And he dreams about the airport.

I have a friend called Sam,
Who has a bear named Pam.
He says he's real cool,
And he enjoys swimming in the pool.

Kim Taylor (9)
Lawns Park Primary School

Going To Bed

Goodnight, sleep tight
Let the wind blow wild.
Goodnight, sleep tight
Let the rain fall on your pane.
With your bed in the corner
And your ted saying, 'Coming to bed?'
Would you like to go outside instead?
As you climb into bed, you close your eyes
Off to Dream Mountain you go.
Shh . . . shh . . .

Jennifer Rasal (7)
Lawns Park Primary School

My Sister Is My Star

My baby sister never stays still,
Sometimes she pretends to be ill.
My baby sister can crawl and walk,
Some people think it's amazing she can talk.
My baby sister is the very best, she's so clever
I think she could do my Year 4 test.
But there's one thing I'd like to say
And I always think it over each day.
I love my sister with all my heart
And I've loved her from the very start.

Jade Kernick (8)
Lawns Park Primary School

My Grandpa

My grandpa is old,
Very old.
His hair is grey and his eyes are weak.
He stutters when he speaks.
He drives my grandma mad
Because at times he can be bad.
Even though he is old,
He has a heart of gold.

Charlotte Rose Sylvester (8)
Lawns Park Primary School

What I Like

A   is for apples as red as strawberries
P   is for pears as green as a field of grass
P   is for peaches as orange as a carrot
L   is for lemons as yellow as the sun
E   is for eggs as white as snow
S   is for sausages that go with a bang!

Tayler-Marie Hackney (8)
Lawns Park Primary School

What I Like

I like
Horse riding
Through the
Green fields.

I like
Gymnastics
When I do
Backflips.

I like
Swimming
When I swim like
A dolphin.

Ellecia Rose McLoughlin (9)
Lawns Park Primary School

My Grandma

My grandma is as wrinkly as a lump of tar.
She smokes like a racing car.
When she plays darts she uses custard tarts
And she makes car parts.
She doesn't like walking
But she loves talking.

Thomas Needham (8)
Lawns Park Primary School

My Grandma

My grandma's skin is as soft as silk.
She's as cuddly as a teddy bear.
When she cuddles me it feels like a warm blanket around me.
When she looks at me her eyes sparkle like a star in the sky.

Ellis Jaques (9)
Lawns Park Primary School

Liberty

My name means Freedom
Freedom to fly
Like the birds up in the sky
That is the way it will always be
Because my name is Liberty.
Free to do as I please
Fly over land or sail the seas
Go round the world, get back for tea
Because my name is Liberty.
Free to travel on the train
Go to Rome or maybe Spain.
All the famous sights to see
Because my name is Liberty.

Liberty Wightman (10)
Lawns Park Primary School

My Cousin

My cousin is as small as a rabbit
And as light as a feather,
He laughs like a hyena
And is as fast as a cheetah.

His eyes sparkle in the night,
And when he's asleep
He's as cute as a kitten,
And as cuddly as a bear.

He's a very cheeky monkey
All the girls think he's funky
He's as tough as nails
But he always protects me!

Sophie Dickson (9)
Lawns Park Primary School

England's Victory!

England were through to the final
They set off onto the coach.
'Off we go,' said the manager.
'We've got a long journey to approach.'

We went into the hotel,
The room was filled with chairs.
I looked in as we booked in
Oh gosh! I've got a few hairs.

We climbed up to the room,
There in the corner lay a Hoover.
What was it for anyway?
I really need an orange soother.

I went to my bed, my head lay on the pillow
'Goodnight, sleep tight, Will,'
As Johnson tucked me in.
You've forgotten to pay your bill.

So we left the city
And off we did go!
Then Clive the manager said,
'We're going to glow.'

We had arrived and we were greeted
As happy as we could be
And soon Australia you'll see that we are England
And all the glory goes to me!

Gideon Ziff (11)
Leeds Grammar School

The Ballad Of Gregory Hick

On a mild day in summer
There was a young man called Gregory Hick
There was grass of green with dewfall
With the loading revolver going click.

Gregory walked out, evil in his eyes
The victim poor Mark Dooley.
There was a clang and then a bang
Gregory was obviously loony.

The next victim was Julie Winter
A young girl of seven.
There was another clang and a bang
And Julie went up to Heaven.

You may wonder how we caught
Young Gregory Hick.
I don't think I should tell you
It could make you sick.

Anyway this young Greg was not the brightest chap
We had him caught with his gun to the head of another
We'd caught him red-handed
His only defendant his brother.

He was sentenced to the penalty of death
And summoned to the electric chair
And with a clang and a bang
Gregory went with a flare.

At the funeral only one person turned up
Even the vicar didn't come
And now it's time to say goodbye
But Gregory scored two, police only one!

Felix Hill (11)
Leeds Grammar School

Tempest Poems

T errible storm
E nding in catastrophe
M ade by Prospero
P rospero the enchanter
E very square foot
S mothered in his magic
T he crew from the ship swam.

T he enchanter pulled a trick
E very man except one
M any thought Alonso's son dead
P eople from the destroyed ship
E ach name Gonzalo, Alonso, Antonio,
S ebastian Ferdinand and more
T hought to have survived the treacherous storm.

T he servant spirit Ariel
E ntwined with Caliban,
M ost ugliest of them all, was
P rospero's slave
E very day Ariel would serve him
S o with two days before its freedom
T he spirit obeys its master.

T rinulo the jester
E ntered Caliban's shelter
M ade out the smell of foul-smelling fish
P rospero watched this all through Ariel's eyes.
E very single step they made
S urveying them closely
T he tempest caused this all.

David Crothers (10)
Leeds Grammar School

The Tempest

T he day when Prospero was exiled a terrible storm occured
E veryone on the battered-up ship believed each other dead
M iranda, the beauty queen falls in love with romantic Ferdinand
P rospero sets an almost impossible challenge to test
                                        Ferdinand's love.
E vil Caliban gets drunk with two twits from the ship
S ome wicked fools try to murder Prospero and King Alonso.
T hen all is well Ariel, Prospero's loyal servant is set free and
                        everyone enjoys life in the future.

Jack Bickler (10)
Leeds Grammar School

The Tempest

T he clever Prospero starts a storm
E nding up crew-tossed on to an isle near early dawn
M iranda and Ferdinand fall in love
P rospero tests by telling to wood shove
E very idiot gets drunk
S ebastian has no chance of ever becoming a monk
T he one and only Prospero loses his magic junk.

William Cracknell (11)
Leeds Grammar School

Tempest

'T was Prospero who started the storm
E ach person drifted onto the shore
M iranda who loved Ferdinand was as bright as dawn
P rospero who was angry and wanted more
E veryone of us will know
S ebastian's plan to kill King Alonso
'T was a happy ending though.

James Bickler (10)
Leeds Grammar School

My Ballad

On the day of the World Cup,
The final that it was,
Many people came to see,
Especially Tony Loz.

He crept towards the pitch,
With the gun in his hand,
He sang as he rang,
The boss as he had planned.

Johnson was about to score,
Just before he was tackled,
But now had passed it to Wilkinson,
As cruel Tony Loz cackled.

He pulled the machine gun,
Out of his jean pocket,
Ready to strike and kill.
Then to run as fast as a rocket!

Gun at the ready,
Finger on trigger,
Wilkinson he was aiming for.
But with the plan still to get bigger.

The gunshot was silenced,
By Johnny's loud scream,
The gasp of the entire crowd,
And Tony's eyes beamed!

But Johnny had not died,
His scream's reason,
Was the drop-kick,
Of this World Cup's season.

England had won,
Johnny filled with pride,
Tony was taken away,
For the judge to decide.

Oliver Lestner (11)
Leeds Grammar School

The Rugby World Cup

It was a freezing cold Saturday morning,
I rubbed the sleep from my eyes,
Dad came in and said,
That for breakfast we're having mince pies.

I went downstairs, on went the TV,
The rugby was starting soon,
I had Coco-Pops without pork chops,
Mum was blowing up a balloon.

England got off to a bad start,
Australia was five-nil up,
Wilkinson scored, no one was bored,
Robinson scored to make us nearer to winning the cup.

The whistle blew, it was half-time,
It was fourteen-five to us,
Everyone thought they couldn't catch up,
The crowd made an excited buzz.

Australia came out with a fighting spirit,
They were determined to win,
It really showed cos they clawed their way back,
And did not get a single sinbin.

There was one minute left, we were winning,
Only by three points,
Unfortunately they got a penalty,
The kicker prepared his leg joints.

Australia wanted Flatley to score,
The ball to fly straight and true,
Unfortunately for us it did,
The England crowd started to boo!

The score in the final was fourteen-all,
It went into extra time,
Clive Woodward shouted at his men,
'To lose now would be a crime!'

Wilkinson scored early,
We were seventeen-fourteen up,
All the players gave a sigh of relief,
England was nearer to winning the cup.

Oh no! Flatley scored again,
Golden points loom,
The score was tied seventeen-all,
For one of us it would be doom.

Johnson broke through their defence,
Dawson took the ball out,
Passed it to Wilkinson who kicked it,
Ref said, 'Goal!' What a shout!

We had won the World Cup,
The first major title in thirty-seven years,
Johnson lifted the cup,
And with it brought tears.

Daniel Saffer (11)
Leeds Grammar School

There Is A Monster Under The Bed

There is a monster under the bed
I can't rest my poor head
All I want to do is sleep
But I'm not getting one little peep

There is a monster under the bed
I called my dad, his name is Fred
I told him what I told you
But he just said that that's not true

There is a monster under the bed
I bet he has not been fed
Do you think that he'll eat me?
I don't want to be his tea

There is a monster under the bed
I called to him, then I said,
'Let's bring this nightmare to an end
I'm not scared, I'll be your friend.'

Zack Sorkin (9)
Leeds Grammar School

My Ballad

Oh, it was a dreadful night,
As Felix Hill knew,
Someone had killed his wife,
And he was going to too!

The victim was his sister,
Whom he loved a lot,
He couldn't believe he was doing it,
When he picked up the pot.

The effect it was terrible,
There was blood everywhere,
When he saw the police come,
He roared like a bear.

He hid beneath the lid of a bin,
As he heard the door open up,
Felix started to get scared,
So he threw a brand new cup.

The police they heard the crash,
Quickly and quietly they moved in,
They found Felix dead on the floor,
With blood in the bin.

And that's the story of Felix,
A murderer who tried to kill,
If he'd escaped he had plans to kill again,
Not his mum but his best friend Bill.

But the police still had a mystery,
Who killed Felix Hill?
They found from their unsure neighbour
It was his girlfriend Jill.

The chief came in sweaty,
And started to say what he saw,
But the bullet got him faster,
As the murderer ran for the door.

No one knows who did it,
Except the brave Chief Lay,
So it still remains a mystery,
To this very day!

David Lee (10)
Leeds Grammar School

The Ballad Of Clive Woodward

The England manager, Clive Woodward,
He was absolutely speechless,
When he was in the tunnel,
He didn't have any stress.

When Jonny scored the winner,
Clive went totally mad,
It was hard to believe and it was almost Christmas Eve,
The Aussies were very sad.

When Clive got his medal,
The crowd gave a huge cheer,
He was so very happy,
Because the trophy was very near.

They all had worked so very hard,
They could now have a rest,
They have now proved
That they are the very best.

The news goes round the world,
China, Japan and Spain,
As they had finished the match,
It was still pouring down with rain.

George Berson (11)
Leeds Grammar School

The Rugby World Cup

At first it was not nail-biting
When Australia scored first
It started to get exciting
When England made a burst

Then started the second half
The players were being admired
The crowd were having a laugh
The players were really tired.

Extra time began
England had a minute to score
Then Wilkinson kicked the ball over
And the crowd started to roar.

Haaris Ahmed (11)
Leeds Grammar School

English Sporting Heroes

You should have seen Jonny 20 seconds from time.
I can bet you know he at least got a dime.
But Beckham has a say
So he didn't have to pay.

Henman was amazing.
His opponent was dazing.
Campbell was like a flash.
So the others paid the cash.

Vaughen was not tubby.
The South Africans were chubby.
Radcliffe kept on going.
The others were slowing.

Jack Goldstone (11)
Leeds Grammar School

War On Terrorism

S addam was with chemicals,
A merica has him now.
D *oh, doh, doh,* Saddam thinks,
D *oh, they're going to kill me.*
A ttacking with chemicals would have been nice,
M an, oh man, that would have been good.

G eorge W Bush,
E lected President of America.
O ut with Saddam,
R *atatat-tat*
G oes the machine gun, killing terrorists,
E nding for Saddam is here.

B in Laden,
I nside, somewhere out there,
N ations against him.

L anding of Americans
A t one mission.
D estroy Bin Laden now,
E nd of the rat is near,
N ow to kill him.

Samuel Rozday (10)
Leeds Grammar School

The Tempest

'T he storms begin!' exiled Prospero commands,
E very ship will be wrecked upon the sands,
M iranda falls in love with Ferdinand,
P rospero tests their loving bonds and
E lsewhere Caliban with sailors planned
S ometime to murder Prospero with his hand,
T he plot is foiled, Ariel is free to roam the land.

Henry Verhees (10)
Leeds Grammar School

Jonny Wilkinson

It was England's turn to win the World Cup
With Wilkinson, Robinson and more
They played a good Australian side
And they did settle that score.

Wilkinson got a few kicks
And Robinson scored a try
But the Australians also scored one too
Though England didn't let many more by.

The noise throughout the stadium
Was as loud as loud can be
The cheering fans sang, 'Swing low'
For England's star, Jonny.

And as the second half progressed
The Aussies chipped away
The lead England once had
Was quickly worn away.

In the dying seconds of extra time
Jonny gets the ball
And with one last spurt of effort
He kicks the winning drop goal.

Harry Fellerman (10)
Leeds Grammar School

The Tempest

'T was without doubt a fine idea,
E ventually it occurred,
M et Miranda did Ferdinand,
P rospero was glad of this,
E ven so he tested,
S o Ferdinand was slave,
'T was true love in the end.

Adnan Memon (11)
Leeds Grammar School

Bonfire Night

Bonfire Night
Is colourful and bright.
The party's loud
With a very big crowd.
Remember Guy Fawkes, remember Guy Fawkes.

Fireworks
Go crashing and bashing.
They swirl
Just like a ballerina's twirl.
Remember Guy Fawkes, remember Guy Fawkes.

The bonfire
Is very hot, rather like a cooking pot.
The flames rise high
Up into the moonlit sky.
Remember Guy Fawkes, remember Guy Fawkes.

Bonfire food
It helps my mood.
It's sticky and yummy
And it fills up my tummy.
Remember Guy Fawkes, remember Guy Fawkes.

Tom Wilcox (9)
Leeds Grammar School

The Tempest

T he one and only Prospero decides to make a tempest.
E ventually a ship came crashing upon the waves, suddenly the ship
   tipped and crashed into the sea and the crew were washed up on
   the island.
M iranda, Prospero's daughter, falls in love with Ferdinand.
P rospero tests Ferdinand's love with Miranda.
E ventually Caliban tries wine with two idiots from the ship.
S tupidly two murder plots to kill Prospero and King Alonso fail.
T he one and only Prospero sets Ariel free and they all live happily
   ever after.

Mark Fuszard (11)
Leeds Grammar School

My Ballad

I woke up in the morning
I looked up at my clock
Oh, my large pantyhose
I fell like a rock

I ran down to the lounge
I jumped and lay on the sofa
I turned it on and learned
How to open a can of soda

It was all equal at the end
They went into extra time
I was jumping around like a mental cow
Then it was the extra time's half-time.

They were still equal, I hated it
But then with five minutes left
They had a ruck, they had to pass
They did, to Jonny, he kicked it on his left.

It was going left of the posts
I thought it was missing
But then the wind caught it
And it went over, the Aussies were hissing.

James Wainman (11)
Leeds Grammar School

My Girlfriend

My girlfriend has short blonde hair,
She's 8 years old and she never cries,
I think she's an angel who'll never die,
She hurts me in my heart,
Plus she pulls me apart,
But now it's all over,
Because I'm seeing Clover.

Joseph Raper (7)
Leeds Grammar School

The Rugby World Cup Final

The 22nd of November,
A date that sticks in your mind.
A day when England rugby players
Left Australia behind.

It was the World Cup Final,
Rugby was the game.
Australia were very good, however
The Wallabies are now tame.

Tiquri and Robinson both scored,
Both were sensational tries.
However, Flatley missed his kick,
England couldn't believe their eyes!

The full time whistle blew,
The score was a draw.
The tension was at a maximum,
There were going to be some more!

Wilkinson got a penalty,
Flatley got one too.
Wilkinson got a drop goal,
The final whistle blew.

England held the Webb Ellis Cup,
The first in the Northern hemisphere.
We saluted them when they got back,
The Webb Ellis Cup was here.

That was how it happened,
A date in English history.
It made an impact on the world,
But most of all on me.

Hugo Govett (11)
Leeds Grammar School

Serving Time

The massive dark door clunked behind them
As they trudged into that terrible place
They line up single file in their regulation uniform
Wishing that they had never been born

They all picked up their bags
And then were led off to their rooms
Nervously getting ready
To begin their eight-year sentence

Then they began their hard work and labour
Rising before dawn for their chores
Before they began their lessons
Which were so much of a bore

As they trudged into the dining room
Holding their noses in dread
There was an awful whiff of cabbage
And they wished that they were dead

When they went for their daily run
Which was fifteen miles long
Five had fainted halfway round
And twelve had got it wrong

The next day the visitors came
And gave them some hugs and kisses
Because they won't see their loved ones again
Not for another twelve weeks

They will have to get used to this
These are only the first days
Of their 8-year sentence
At . . . boarding school.

Dominic Brooke (10)
Leeds Grammar School

Cricket

Cricket is a good game,
Football is not the same,
Sachin Tendulkar is a good batsman,
Shane Warne is coming back from his 2 years' ban,
If India loses the game,
The Captain gets the blame,
When the players have their lunch,
They have a jolly good munch,
In cricket the players can't stand on the pitch,
When they get hurt they might have a stitch.

Adithya Sreedharan (7)
Leeds Grammar School

Tigers

T igers are the best
I t's the cat of the century
G rowl and roar is what they do
E ating all the animals that they see
R ipping them up one by one
S taring at me, I must run!

Freddie Machin (7)
Leeds Grammar School

Jungle Playground

In the jungle it's so loud,
Parrots and monkeys staring proud.
In the jungle the monkey swings,
To his family bananas he brings.
I wish the jungle was my playground,
I'd love to have all my friends round.

Adam Ross (7)
Leeds Grammar School

My Dog Bill

I have a dog and his name is Bill
He doesn't know how to sit still.

In the streets and the park I'd give him a walk
And when we are out, here is how I talk.

'Bill, Bill, please sit still
Obey me, Bill, you're making me ill.

Bill, Bill, go fetch that stick
Hurry up, Bill, do be quick.

Bill, Bill, throw the ball
Come on, Bill, get off the wall.

Bill, Bill, stop it please
Stop eating that man's mushy peas.

No, Bill, no! Not on the floor
The man will have to buy some more.

Bill Mcgregor, get over here now
There's going to be a massive row.

I'm sorry, Bill, for telling you off
I think it's because I'm full of a cough.'

Bill Mcgregor died eventually
At the massive age of 20.

Henry Richmond (10)
Leeds Grammar School

Winter

In winter, cold and dark,
I'm not allowed to play in the park.
At night there's no light,
It's hard to make someone feel bright.

Daniel Bello (8)
Leeds Grammar School

On My Birthday

On my birthday I wake up early,
run downstairs and open my presents.
I play with them happily,
I sit down tiredly next to my presents
and think about my party cheerily.
I end the day with thoughts of all my lovely
little presents given to me
on my precious day by lovely
friends and family.

Harmandeep Tatla (9)
Leeds Grammar School

Going Skiing

S tepping into my ski boots
K icking the snow at my sister!
I 'm going skiing!
I nto the lift I jump
N obody on the slopes
G oing very fast down the hill.

Max Elgot (7)
Leeds Grammar School

Weather

We like it when the sun comes out,
But in Africa there might be drought,
We don't like it when it rains,
But in Africa it grows their grain,
Everybody likes it when it snows,
I get on my sledge and say, 'Go, go, go!'

James Groom (7)
Leeds Grammar School

The Supernatural

Out there, in the darkness of space
Lies the supernatural,
Far, far beyond the stars
Lies the supernatural,
Odd and wondrous though they are
They are the supernatural,
Some have one eye, some have three
But they are the supernatural,
Some are violet, some are green
But they're still the supernatural,
They all live in odd places, though
They are the supernatural,
So next time you stare up into the sky
Remember the supernatural.

James Roberts (8)
Leeds Grammar School

A Holiday In Austria

Being in Austria is quite fun,
In big ski boots you can't run,
It is a bit hard to ski,
But it is just fun for me,
Running through the really thick snow,
I'll get so, so wet I know!

Marius Tirlea (8)
Leeds Grammar School

Rugby

Rugby, rugby is so tough
But it's also kind of rough
I got the ball and was so fast
That I scored a try
For my team at last!

Joel Groom (7)
Leeds Grammar School

The Vicious Eagle

An eagle is a beautiful sight,
But better when in full flight,
With its feathers reflecting the sunlight.

An eagle is a bird of prey,
Which goes hunting every day,
In search of food it can slay.

Bald, golden or black and white,
Soaring high in the bright sunlight,
Majestic in its lofty flight.

Majestic, elegant bird of prey,
Wingtips catching the last sun's ray,
But rarely seen in the wild today.

Tim Ruston (8)
Leeds Grammar School

My Baby Cousin

She said she would let me hold it.
I felt so nervous I didn't know what to say.

I gave it a go
But my cheeks started to glow bright red,
I even began to sweat.

They took a picture with a snap and a flash
Oh no! I've blinked
But out it came in a dash.

I felt relieved it was all over
Phew, she didn't cry or roll over!

Toby Ziff (8)
Leeds Grammar School

Planet Poem

There are nine planets
In our solar system
They spin round the sun
But I'm not going to list 'em

The sun, the moon
And all the stars
Do you believe
There's life on Mars?

Asteroid rings
That float in space
Which are marvelled at by
The human race

Nine spherical objects
That move around our sun
Pluto is the ninth away
And Mercury number one

The Earth spins on its axis
In the Milky Way
It takes 24 hours
Which equals one Earth day

We orbit the sun
Not the other way
So let's make that clear
And the time that it takes
Is one human year.

Jonathan Castle (9)
Leeds Grammar School

My Grandma

A very big family my grandma had,
There was Uncle John, Auntie Doris and, of course, my dad.
There were others whose names I cannot recall,
Some thin, some fat, some short, some tall.

They played lots of games with balls and with bats,
Sometimes they dressed up in coats and strange hats.
In summer, in winter and all through the year
They sang lots of songs whilst the grown-ups drank beer.

As they sang on all through the night,
Some folks thought there might be a terrible fight.
My grandma was the youngest of them all
But for her age she was very small.
A happy child sure was she,
Nevertheless, as small as a pea.

Henry Dalton (8)
Leeds Grammar School

Bonfire Night

Bonfire Night is the best time of year,
Fireworks shoot into the sky,
The sky becomes a luminous glow,
Dazzling lights everywhere,
Crackling fireworks heard all over.

Bonfire Night is the best time of year,
The bonfire's sparks shoot out in all directions,
Giving light to all around it,
Everyone huddles near it to keep warm,
The heat of it warms up their hearts.

As it does mine.

Max Rooney (9)
Leeds Grammar School

Babysitters

I've heard all about them,
They guzzle your sweets,
And all your nice treats,
Plus they hog the TV all night
Despite all your shouting and screaming.

They boss you all around,
And think they're great,
I just want to hit 'em with a dinner plate,
But it got worse by the second for
Sally came to stay.

Do I really need a babysitter
When they go off to the flicks?
I'm not a boy, I'm now thirty-six!
I think they're being unfair
They're going into overcare!

Joseph Martin (9)
Leeds Grammar School

The Vulture

He rips the flesh from rabbits' heads,
And takes the smaller birds from their beds,
Towards his prey, carefully he treads.

Down to his prey he quickly swoops,
And when he catches it, with joy he hoots,
And afterwards towards him his family groups.

And after that they rip it apart,
Down at the feet is where they start,
And their favourite bit is obviously the heart.

David Swarbrick (9)
Leeds Grammar School

Young Writers - Once Upon A Rhyme Leeds

The PlayStation

The PlayStation drives my mum mad,
Makes my dad very sad,
But is it so bad,
That it makes me very glad?

The PlayStation whirrs all night,
Dad says it ruins my sight,
Mum says, 'Switch on the light,'
And instead my sister says, 'Go and fly your kite!'

The PlayStation is lots of fun,
The hamster watches me like I am dumb,
My mum says I should go for a run,
But I can't possibly until this game is done!

My dad wants me to help him in the garden,
But this level is a very hard one,
And the only way I will have won,
Is if I carry on with my machine gun.

My mum wants me to eat my dinner,
And I really want to be a winner,
My tummy keeps on getting thinner,
But my face is still a huge big grinner.

The PlayStation is a wonderful invention,
It helps me with factual retention,
It takes a lot of my attention,
And sometimes causes me detention!

Christopher Mellor (9)
Leeds Grammar School

Super-Sub

It was a lovely day to play,
For the final game in May.

The boys were all ready,
And they started very steady.

The Leeds Grammar School boys were losing,
Their teacher thought they were snoozing.

At half-time it was one-nil,
And then Jonny was horribly ill.

Daniel, the substitute, came on,
And then the Leeds Grammar School team shone.

With a rush up the wing,
The supporters began to cheer and sing.

And yippee! The ball had gone in!

The final whistle was about to go,
The opposition were looking extremely slow.

Daniel was looking redder and redder,
And suddenly . . . there came his header!

The battle had gone,
And Leeds Grammar School had won!

The boys got the cup,
And then . . . Daniel woke up!

Daniel Davidson (8)
Leeds Grammar School

Winter Days

W histling winds blow powerfully into your face,
 I cy ponds like a mirror, the sun is shining with grace,
N ipping, cold, biting snow, drives hard into your nose,
T errifying waves of hailstorms coming down in droves.
E xcited little children make snowmen, having fun,
R esting over Christmas, the year is almost done.

George Lestner (8)
Leeds Grammar School

Where Do They Go?

Where do teachers go, after school?
On Thursday night is it pool?
On Monday do they go home in a chunky jeep,
Or mark our work while half asleep?

Where do our parents go, after work?
Out for a spin in their Merc?
Do they go to a pub for a drink,
Or stay at home by the kitchen sink?

Where do the children go, at the weekend?
Do they help their dad to something mend?
Or do they play on the PlayStation all day,
Or play outside like it's the middle of May?

Edward Pellow (8)
Leeds Grammar School

Grandma

My grandma is as caring as the sun
She has silky hair like a spider's web
She sleeps like a log with my very big grandad
Sometimes she tells me tales about a scary witch
But best of all I go and sleep at her house
She is so cuddly like a teddy bear
She doesn't drink beer like my grandad
She gives me chocolates and always gives me the bigger piece
Sometimes we bake buns with chocolate on top
We go to town and she buys food and might buy me a toy
We also go to the theatre and watch scary movies
And in the scary bits she will squeeze my hand
But best of all I love her.

Joe Mitchell (9)
Leeds Grammar School

Christmas Tree

In a
Cold, frosty night,
Stood a tall
Green Christmas tree,
With sparkling stars.
The long stem stood
Bravely in the snow.
I dressed it up with
Coloured papers and
Luminous lights,
All green and glowing bright.
White snowflakes on the leaves,
Looked like shimmering trinkets.
All it tried to do was to spread
The message of love and happiness.

Oishik Raha (8)
Leeds Grammar School

A Midsummer Picnic

'Today we're going to have a picnic,'
'Mummy, what is a tick?'
'A tick is a kind of bug.'
'Mummy, I want a hug!'

'Now I know you are all teens,
But please do not eat the beans,
And I know you're in a pram,
But don't eat all the ham.'

'Please try not to stutter,
If you want some butter,
If I ring this little bell,
You can have some caramel.'

Andrew Hooley (9)
Leeds Grammar School

Gran

My gran is sweet as icing on a cake,
But as she's old, sometimes she can't always stay awake,
Always smiling and very merry,
Particularly when she's had a sherry

She's very good at Sunday lunches,
The room is quiet as the table munches,
Then afterwards we often play,
Me and my cousin always want to stay

But later on we have to go,
Often we cry and say, 'No, no, no.'
We always shout, 'Please can we stay?'
To which she replies, 'No, kids, but you can always come back
another day!'

William Lax (8)
Leeds Grammar School

Christmas

Tinsel shines,
Tinsel glitters like a disco light,
And tinsel twirls like a snake around the tree.
The angel or star stands proudly on top of the tree,
The lights glowing brightly,
The ornaments remind my family of past Christmases.
Under the tree are surprises
Just
Waiting
For us to
See them.

Euan Findlater (8)
Leeds Grammar School

The Scenery Of Greenery

The scenery of greenery
Has all sorts of wonderful things,
With lovely green trees,
So bright yellow bees.

In the morning sun
Everybody was having fun,
But only when the work was done
Did everyone go for a run.

During the day
When they saw the fellow,
Did he then say,
'Let's go play in the meadow.'

In the open field
While children played,
Parents were having picnic meals
While the sun fades.

Shivraj R Patel (9)
Leeds Grammar School

I'd Like To Fly

I'd like to fly
Up in the sky
Way, way up high
And see the birds go by

I'd like to fly with the bees
And smell the flowers in the breeze
Through the misty air, over the seas
And solve the pirate mysteries.

Christopher Wilkinson (8)
Leeds Grammar School

Midnight Light

Winter, winter, glorious winter,
Glistening in the midnight light,
When day begins, children play,
Making snowmen all the day.

A blizzard starts, the children run,
But the snowmen stay, cold and wet,
A slushy morning greets their sight,
But the crunchy snow they don't forget.

Max Swycher (8)
Leeds Grammar School

Summer

The salty sea slaps strongly
on the sandy shore.
The scorching sun slowly shrivels
the sensitive sunflowers.
Slumbering spirits sunbathe silently
on sleepy Sundays.

William Mason (8)
Leeds Grammar School

Winter

Winter, winter
Glorious winter
When will you come?
I've been waiting all year long
And now this season has begun
Snow is white like cloud
But when it's gone
I sing a song
This is wrong.

Jake Sorkin (8)
Leeds Grammar School

I Wish I Could Be A Football Star

I wish I could be a football star,
With the other players and the car.
Be on the pitch with the crowd,
Make people shout and make me proud.

I wish I could be a football star,
Go away and be really far.
I will score loads of goals,
The news I hope will reach the Poles.

I wish I could be a football star,
Go with my mates to the bar.
I will go have 8 pints every day,
I really hope I won't have to pay.

Neil Saha (8)
Leeds Grammar School

A Football Game

'Did you hear
There is a football game this year?'
'We can have fun,
Even though there is no sun.'

'It's not very far,
So we don't need to go by car.'
'We don't need to ride our bikes,
But we can if we like.'

'If the match finishes early, oh how lucky,
Because we'll be able to go to Kentucky.'
'So see you on Saturday at half-past eight,
And we'll meet at the stadium gate.'

Yona Knight-Wisdom (8)
Leeds Grammar School

Ancient Greeks

The ancient Greeks were amazing,
The Spartans strong but cruel,
The Athenians kind and loving,
The Thebans always searching for food.

The ancient Greeks were amazing,
And time and time again,
They fought and won battles.
But they came to a sticky end.
The Romans defeated Archimedes,
From then the Greeks were doomed,
Greece became Roman property
And a new future loomed.

Stephen Jones (9)
Leeds Grammar School

Winter

In winter people stand and shiver,
And the coldness makes them quiver.
Dogs are howling in the freezing night,
Children start a snowball fight.

Families sliding on their sledges,
Frost glistens on nearby hedges.
On the ground there's sparkly snow,
The soil is hard and nothing can grow.

I like winter when the days are bright,
Especially when there's a lot of white!

Thomas Fuller (8)
Leeds Grammar School

Summer Holidays

I'm feeling excited,
the summer holidays have come.
I'm like a can of Coke I've shaken and shaken,
that's ready to explode.

I'm looking forward to fun and want to
run! Run! Run!
I'm like a Catherine wheel on Bonfire Night
whizzing around and around.

I'm imagining the sensation of cold, wet
sand on my feet,
like splashing on my face with icy cold waves.

Football, cricket, anything else on offer?
Clubs! Clubs! Clubs!
I'm fully charged like my
remote controlled car.

Picnics too, all my favourites,
taste better on ground.
But, it's only winter now so I'll
keep all my excitement canned!

Adam Javeed (9)
Leeds Grammar School

Winter

Winter, winter, snowflakes fall,
'Mother, Father, may we go out?' the children call.
'Wrap up tight so the frost doesn't bite,
But be inside before moonlight.'

Children play in the snow,
While they have freezing toes.
Hats and gloves don't do the trick,
As all the snow sticks.

Winter comes but then it goes,
The snow has gone and so have all the woes.

Sohail Akhtar (8)
Leeds Grammar School

A Winter's Day

Winter is here and snow is falling on the ground
making a carpet of white snow.
Footprints of animals are visible on the ground,
making a trail for someone to follow.

The trees are bare waiting for snow to come and cover them.
When the snow comes the trees will glisten and sparkle like diamonds.

Icicles hang like fangs from the branches and rooftops of houses.
They drip, drip, drip when the sun comes out.

The nights are long and the days are short,
so hungry birds have little time to search for food in the bitter cold,
bleak weather.
Other animals are hibernating because it is cold
and there is no food around.

All the ponds are frozen over with ice and it shines like glass.
Some people skate and make swirly patterns on the ice.

Children go sledging in the crunchy, cold snow
wearing woolly hats and scarves to keep them warm.
They laugh and squeal with delight as they slide
and tumble to the bottom of the hill.

People dare not go out into the cold and frosty day,
and they sit in front of their warm fires eating hot soup.

When spring eventually comes the snow melts into water,
and all the plants and animals wake up
and come out of their winter sleep.

William Johnson (9)
Leeds Grammar School

The Ballad Of Jonny Wilkinson

Jonny Wilkinson, the hero of the semi-final
Scoring 24 points, winning the game.
Out England came on a dull Saturday night
17-all with half a minute left,
Jonny Wilkinson going for fame.

The scrum-half got the ball out of the scrum,
Passed it to Jonny,
Who tried to drop the goal.
He hit the ball, then dropped to the floor like a demolished wall,
The ball went through the posts and Jonny did a forward roll.

Everyone went wild
And Clive Woodward did too,
The Aussies weren't happy,
So they said, *'Boooo!'*

The fans screamed with joy,
Their faces painted red and white,
Martin Johnson collected the trophy
Standing at his full height.

Joe Barnett (10)
Leeds Grammar School

Autumn

Autumn has come, the leaves change colour,
Leaves fall from the trees which become less fuller.
On the ground they make a bed,
From the darkest brown to the brightest red.
Up above the birds flock by
To warmer climates, we stand and sigh.
All the flowers have shrivelled and died,
It's like they have gone on holiday to hide.

Drew Walker (9)
Leeds Grammar School

Monsters And Fears

When I went to the toilet when I was only three,
My father said if I stayed too long a monster would get me.

I grew up and grew some more and then I was nearly four,
My sister said to me, 'There is a ghost behind the door.'

When I walked to school with Teddy (my best friend)
He said if I stepped on cracks I would meet a sticky end.

When I went to university the professor said to me,
If I did not study hard, I'd be swinging from a tree.

When I got an accounting job my boss said to I,
'If you do not charge them right, you will surely die.'

When I got married, my lovely wife said to me,
'If you do not kiss me I will sting you like a bee.'

For all my life I followed their advice . . .
But then Mum said, 'You should be more afraid of mice.

For mice can bite and nibble,
Don't listen to all this drivel!'

James Markham (10)
Leeds Grammar School

Ricky The Baby

Ricky the baby was very cute,
I took him down the water chute,
His mum was watching with a frown
As I held him upside down.

Ricky squirmed and wriggled,
I just laughed and giggled,
I am fond of Ricky,
But looking after him is very tricky.

David Woon (8)
Leeds Grammar School

Life

It's such a hard game to play,
Such a hard thing to work out,
Such a hard ride to go on,
Life.

It's a budding journey with highs and lows,
It's a roller coaster ride,
For all your life,
My life, my life.

Life,
Marriages, children, death,
Life is those things and much more,
Life, oh life.

Life is a big world as you can see above
With a price tag that money cannot buy,
So do not destroy it.
Live life, life, life, oh life.

My life has been one big show
And it's nearly all over.
I've two sons, one daughter,
My dearest wife I treasure to my heart.
I've kept this poem all my
Life.

Leo Brosh (8)
Leeds Grammar School

The Eagle

He rounds the cliffs looking for prey
Soaring and diving in the bright sunrays,
When he spies a mouse hiding in the hay.

Hovering above the steep cliff track,
Then swiftly diving into attack,
Sharp talons stabbing into its back.

Sam Fellerman (9)
Leeds Grammar School

The Night's Eye

The sun sets,
Lets the moon start the night,
Like a night duty,
Destroys daylight.

The moon shines,
Blinds the eye,
Like a laser
In the sky.

The moon flies,
Tries to beat the sun,
Like a race
For fun.

The moon dips,
Flips under the light,
Like a blanket,
Restarts daylight.

Thomas Smedley (9)
Leeds Grammar School

The Night's Eye

The sun sets
Lets the moon rise
Like a light
With a nice surprise.

The moon shines
Blinds the eye
Like a laser
In the sky.

The moon goes
Blows away the dark
Like a balloon
Blowing away from its mark.

Stephen Hall (9)
Leeds Grammar School

The Magpie

Even when I wake up at dawn
He's hopping around on the lawn;
Trying to peck at the corn.

His feathers are black and white,
Black as black as night;
He's looking for a fight.

He always comes in a pair;
If there's something to steal then beware;
He doesn't seem to care.

Ben Lambert (8)
Leeds Grammar School

A Winter Poem

W et lakes turn to ice
 I cicles as thin and as sharp as a sword
N umb fingers warming by the fire
T rees shed their leaves on the floor
E verything covered in snow
R udolf wrapped up warm in the stable.

Robert Coates (9)
Leeds Grammar School

Winter

Winter is coming, so be aware, because
the puddles will soon be very icy.
The temperature will rarely rise above freezing
so wrap up nice and warm.
I love the wintertime.

The snow will soon start to fall, lovely, white and soft.
The choir sings in the streets, as the robins fly overhead.
All the trees so colourful, I really do love wintertime.

Matthew Gunnee (9)
Leeds Grammar School

Dragon Extinction

They could have lived a long time ago,
No one knows, no one knows,
Are they a legend? Are they extinct?
I don't know.

In my mind I think of them,
Sharp teeth, pointy ears,
Scaly skin, as thick as a brick,
Shiny red wings as thick as a wall,
Brown body, heavy, strong as well.

They are really big and tough, as strong as an ox,
Spiky tail, nice and long,
Extremely fast, watch out they might come to you.
It's a dragon!

Stuart Roney (8)
Leeds Grammar School

Lonely Castle

She travelled through the moonlight,
Underneath stars and trees.
Suddenly she stopped at such a sight,
A home for kings and queens.
But yet not just any home,
'Twas a home of magic!
With fairies flitting in the sky, with fluffy clouds of foam
And many beautiful mermaids in the moat.
She knocked upon the thick wooden door,
But no one seemed to answer,
Then out of nowhere something hit the floor
With a *bang* and a *crash* but still no one answered.
She walloped the door hard this time.
'I know you're in there, don't ignore me!'
Still no one descended to her.
Fuming she strode off!

Caitlin McManus (10)
Miles Hill Primary School

The Runaway Explorer

From out of the dark, dark forest,
Came a woman riding upon her horse.
She was on a quest,
To look for the best,
The best life she could ever wish for.

She soon came across a palace,
(An abandoned one at that!)
The only thing that was left inside,
Was an old and raggy mat.

She showed herself around,
While outside in the palace grounds,
Her greyish black horse,
Ran with such a force,
At an innocent little cat!

Suddenly out of the woods,
Came an army of knights,
Who barged into the palace,
And turned on the lights.

The woman felt frightened and nervous,
So she ran out of the palace,
And jumped on her horse,
And galloped all the way home!

Jennifer Wright (11)
Miles Hill Primary School

The Midnight Horror

The sky turns into darkness,
As the moon begins to rise,
There he stands waiting,
In the middle of the night.

He wanders around the forest,
And he's never out in the day,
If anyone dares to go in,
They will never come out again.

A young man goes in,
And he finds the cottage,
He walks up to the door and he knocks loudly,
'Hello! Hello!'
But no one answers him,
He knocks again even louder!
Bang! Bang!

'Hello,' but still no one answers him,
'Maybe no one is in,' he says loudly,
And finally gives up,
And the sound of his voice gets quieter,
And slowly disappears.

Ashleigh White (11)
Miles Hill Primary School

Here He Is

He ran and ran all day
He ran and ran all night
He ran and ran all year
He didn't have any fear
He was very near.

He is here, he is here.

They ran, they ran
Up the spooky stairs
They left him some chocolate eclairs
They'd hidden in the cupboard
They wrote on the board,
'Go away
Fly away
Run away
Just get away'

And he did
He ran and ran all day
He ran and ran all night
He ran and ran all month
He ran and ran all year
Now he did have fear.

Jade Newton (11)
Miles Hill Primary School

Shadow Of Darkness

The moonlight shone on the darkness,
as a shadow crept by the house.
A mysterious man in moonlight
whispered to a hooting owl,
'Call with your hoot if anyone answers,
and I shall be back by noon.'
And so the owl listened as the shadow was
feeding his horse.
Soon the footsteps of inside met the staircase,
then tiptoed down the stairs,
The owl hooted with fright, which made the
shadow rush through the field,
to see who'd opened the door.
But a scare was waiting for the shadow,
for out jumped a man with a knife,
and no one knows what happened,
on that
disastrous
spooky *night!*

Natalie Maciag (9)
Miles Hill Primary School

The Creepy Cottage

'Hello, anyone here?' asked the lonely tourist
clanking the knocker on the door.
She only heard the hooting of an owl
in the background of the night.
'Hello? My car has broken down
and I can't get home, please can you help me?'
There was nothing but silence that
came to the lonely tourist's ears.
'Is there anybody here?' shouted the lonely tourist
banging on the dark wooden door
'Help!' roared the lonely tourist.
The owl hooted back to her
'Nnnnnoooo!' she screamed and fell to her knees
and broke down in tears.
The lonely tourist lay down on the
moonlit porch and cried herself to sleep.

Amber McCall (9)
Miles Hill Primary School

Boys And Girls

Boys shout, girls giggle,
Pencils write, squiggle, squiggle,
Get it wrong, cross it out,
Bell rings, all out!

Boys slap, girls play,
Nursery children run away,
Get some paint, do some art,
Put some merits on the chart!

Boys bad, girls good,
Rain falls, put up your hood,
Time for home, time for tea,
Time to go to bed, that's me!

Georgia Wade (7)
Our Lady's School

School Day

Boys shout, girls giggle,
Pencils write, squiggle, squiggle,
Get it wrong, cross it out,
Bell rings, all out!

Boys play, girls clap,
Little children have a nap,
Joe's feet hit the ground,
Miss Hodgson walks around.

Boys read, girls write,
Laura gets in a horrible fright,
Turn on the light, bright, bright, bright,
Then the day turns into night.

Boys drink, girls eat,
Some of the teachers have smelly feet,
Some of us like to cheat,
Bullies we don't like to meet.

Boys are bad, girls are good,
They always listen when they should.
Aaron's foot goes *thud! Thud! Thud!*
I'd go to the shop if I could!

Jessica Beaumont (7)
Our Lady's School

About Me

Hi, my name is Rebecca Hind,
I'm 10 and very cool,
On my skateboard I do grind,
I go to the best school.

My neighbour's cat is very fab,
I like to play out with my mates,
I have a Nike black hat,
On Emmerdale I like the Tates!

Rebecca Hind (10)
Our Lady's School

A Busy Day

Boys shout, girls giggle,
Pencils write, squiggle, squiggle,
Get it wrong, cross it out,
Bell rings, all out!

Boys clap, girls have a nap,
Babies crawl, mums and dads call,
Aunties tap, uncles rap,
Dogs bark and run to the park!

Boys are tall, girls are small,
Toddlers run around and then hit the ground,
The mums call, the dogs bark,
Come in now, it's nearly dark!

Laura Hirst (7)
Our Lady's School

All About Me

My name is Shauna, I am 10,
My best game is Twister,
My friends are Sally, Sam and Ben
I have a younger sister.

I like to play in mud that's wet,
My sister thinks it's cool,
I have a big dog as my pet,
My mum and dad they rule.

I like to go to school and learn,
I have a fun-filled time,
We have to learn to take our turn,
And stand in a straight line.

Shauna Blackburn (10)
Our Lady's School

A Poem About Me And My Bike

Sometimes I like to play outside,
I play out on my bike.
It's purple and has beads on it,
It's the bike my friends like.

It's a wonderful bike to ride,
I play with it outside.
When I play on my bike outside,
I laugh and split my sides.

My bike is big and colourful,
It's cool and also fast,
And for my bike I am grateful,
When I race I come last.

Danielle Langstaff (9)
Our Lady's School

Me And My Friends

Me and my friends like to play out,
We joke, we laugh, we run,
We sing and laugh and dance about,
We have a lot of fun.

I go swimming a lot of times,
I go almost each day,
I like making a lot of rhymes,
My favourite month is May.

My nan and grandad have a dog,
We play with it a lot,
My auntie's daughter has a frog,
It has a big red spot.

Cathy-Marie Sykes (10)
Our Lady's School

What I Like And Don't

I eat strawberry candyfloss,
At school I write with a pen,
When old I want to be a boss,
But now I'm only 10.

Me and Mum like going to shops,
I love to eat thin chips,
I love to eat those rainbow drops,
I don't like to eat pips.

I don't like sleeping in the dark,
Once I had a pet mouse,
When it is day, I like the park,
I have a big posh house.

Jodie Pawson (10)
Our Lady's School

All About Me

I like to watch a DVD,
I sit with all my mates,
I also like to watch TV,
And stay up very late.

I like to watch The Premiership,
My favourite team is Leeds,
My favourite food is really chips,
By my mum gives me swede.

I like to play with all my friends,
I ride upon my bike,
When I'm out I like to pretend
One of my friends is Mike.

Jack Wall (10)
Our Lady's School

All About Me - Just Me!

I really hate avocado,
I am 10 years of age,
Nickname is Nelly Furtado!
My pet lives in a cage!

I really love to sing and dance,
I try to keep the beat,
Round and round I sing and prance,
I get up on my feet!

So my behaviour may be bad,
Mum says I have good looks,
I might get crazy, sad or mad!
Keep me in your good books!

I put effort into my looks,
I do love to eat sweets!
Me and mum are like chefs or cooks,
I get my sweets form Pete's!

Chanelle Sefton (10)
Our Lady's School

My Life

My dream is to be a pop star,
I like fame and fortune,
To go on holiday afar,
Sounds like a super tune.

I can't just leave my friends behind,
They're very close to me,
My friends are very nice and kind,
Without them I can't be.

I'm happy as a little kid,
My life is really fun,
Out in the snow I like to skid,
My favourite cake's a bun.

Emma Swithenbank (9)
Our Lady's School

My Favourite Things

Music I like to listen to,
Outkast is very cool;
My brother likes to listen too,
But I think he's a fool.

My favourite food is fish and chips,
I like it for my tea;
I like the flavour on my lips,
It tastes lovely to me.

I like a team called The Rhinos,
I think they are the best;
The top player is Rob Burrows,
Better than all the rest.

My favourite subject is maths,
My second best is art;
After school I enjoy a bath,
I think I'm very smart.

I am only in primary,
Get me out of here please;
I like to eat so much dairy,
My favourite one is cheese.

Robert Halls (10)
Our Lady's School

A Poem About Me

My name is Conor and I'm ten,
I like to jump and hurry,
My little cousin is called Ben,
My favourite food is curry.

I like to play out with my friends,
We like to play football,
I wish our fun would never end,
My friend is very tall.

Conor Burnell (10)
Our Lady's School

Matteo's Life

I am happy when I play games,
I am sad when I fall,
Then I get up and look at planes,
I like to climb a wall.

I like to go out on my bike,
I don't like to fall,
But I like my best friend called Mike
Who has got a bad cough.

I like to go to bed and sleep,
I have very nice dreams,
I dream of things by counting sheep,
I like the bright moonbeams.

I wake up on a school morning,
And I get my breakfast,
In class I am sometimes yawning,
At playtime I run fast.

I go home and play with my mates,
And play with my brother,
I go home and walk through my gate,
I'm met by my mother.

I go to bed once more again,
And have a nice big dream,
In the dream my name is called Ben,
And I see the moonbeam.

And I wake up again right now,
And go and get some clothes,
I go to school and see a cow,
I jump and touch my toes.

Matteo Longoni (10)
Our Lady's School

My Life

My name is Danielle L Green
I like to have some fun
I enjoy watching Mr Bean
I like to have a bun.

When I am outside playing football
In the garden at my home
I play with my best friend called Paul
We try to hit the gnome.

In my bedroom when I'm asleep
Outside when it is dark
I am awoken by a jeep
Driving towards the park.

I am very scared of the dark
I cry if lights go off
When lights go off I hear a bark
Sometimes I see white froth.

Danielle Green (10)
Our Lady's School

Just Me

I am a girl called Laura-Jade,
I am just ten years old,
A pretty birthday cake I made
I like to collect gold.

I like to go out on my bike,
My favourite food is rice,
There are lots of things in life I like,
But I'm not fond of mice.

I go out shopping in the town,
And spend my dad's money,
We go all round, up hill and down,
And then eat bread and honey.

Laura Quigley (10)
Our Lady's School

My Life

I went to visit Paul and Sal
We went right to the park
They are my best and favourite pals
We heard a big dog bark.

My dog's called Pip and he is big
My brown cat is called Marge
Dogs like to run and play and dig
My cat is very large.

I like to run, skip, walk, jog and play
I play and I sweat bad
I can run and skip and play all day
It makes me really glad.

I hate the food called broccoli
I hate the food called fish
Although they're healthy food for me
They are a bad taste.

Kieran Bedford (10)
Our Lady's School

Food!

Food, food, wonderful food
here, there and everywhere.
Food, food, wonderful food
I don't like bananas or pears.

Junk food, junk food, wonderful junk food
chocolate, lollies and sweets.
Junk food, junk food, wonderful junk food
just what I need for a midnight feast.

Fruit, fruit, sweet and sour fruit
apples, pears and plums.
Fruit, fruit, sweet and sour fruit
and it's good, according to mums.

Jordan Gee (11)
Our Lady's School

About Me

I like to play with mates all day,
My father is old aged,
I like to go to school and work,
My best friend is called Paige.

When I'm at school I learn and play,
In mornings we read books,
I lose my pencil everyday,
And then I have to look.

When it's time to go home at three,
I go home in the car,
When I'm at home I watch TV,
I hug and kiss Grandpa.

In the garden I play football,
I play with my brother,
And I go shopping at the stall,
And I love my mother.

Gina Bentley (9)
Our Lady's School

Leeds FC

Smithy scored yesterday
The crowd shouted, 'Hooray!'
The ball hit the wide open net,
It flew through the air as fast as a jet
The crowds shouted, 'Come on, Leeds,
Another goal is what we need!'

When we were ready to kick off again
The weather got bad and it started to rain
The ref said, 'Come on let's call it a day!'
So I went home with family on the bumpy train.

Connor Lindsay (11)
Our Lady's School

The Things I Like

I like running
I like ball
But if it's muddy
I'll always fall.

I like drawing
I think it's fun
My dad's a teacher
And I'm his son.

I like swimming
It is great
Always with Liam
For he's my mate.

I like seas
Boats are rowing
For this is the day
I wrote my poem.

Louis Gallagher (10)
Our Lady's School

My Life And About Me

My name is Imogen, I'm ten,
I like to ride my bike,
Up and down the hill and back again,
My brother is called Mike.

I like to go swimming a lot,
I like to watch TV,
I like it when the sun is hot,
And I swim in the sea.

Imogen Wigglesworth (10)
Our Lady's School

The Deep Blue Sea

When I grow up I'd like to be
As free as a mermaid in the sea.
I would like to swim all day
And watch the fish as they play.

The big blue whale
See him go
And the sea horses
As they dance to and fro.

The dolphins swim
Around the old wrecked ark
Watching carefully
For the great white shark.

Beneath the waves
In the big blue kingdom
The oysters watch
With their pearls of wisdom.

Alesha Smith (10)
Our Lady's School

My Family

My mum is the best, she is fun
She likes her cooking, I like her buns
She loves her art and hates my mess
When it comes to family she's in my nest.

My dad is cool, he's the only one I've got
When it comes to cooking he's in the pot
He's really, really weird and makes up silly words
He's a computer nut and we call him a nerd.

My brother, he loves his sport
He gets seasick even at the port
He's really, really chatty and always makes friends first
And sometimes he's really kind, I think that boy is cursed.

Chloe Wilkes (11)
Our Lady's School

Dreams

Dreams, dreams, all around,
You can't see them in the air,
You can't see them on the ground.

You can have them in the day,
You can have them at night,
You don't need your eyes,
Imagination is your sight.

Dreams, dreams,
They can take you anywhere.
You can feel happy and bouncy,
Or you can feel shocked and scared.

Ride the dreams' roller coaster if you dare,
You might get a welcome,
You might get a beware!

Tara Greaves (10)
Our Lady's School

School Time!

Wake up! Wake up! It's time to go to school,
We all must learn not to be a fool.

Line up! Line up! The bell has gone,
First lesson, let's all sing a song.

Science, history, English and maths,
We love to read and draw some graphs.

Dinner time! Dinner time! It's time to eat,
Chips, pizza, yum-yum, then a sweet.

Playtime! Playtime! We all have fun and talk,
On our way back, we don't run, we must walk.

Home time! Home time! Hip! Hip! Hooray!
School's out, then we're back for another day.

Ann-Marie Reed (11)
Our Lady's School

A Day In The Life Of Tom

Look at me now I want to play
Don't tell me to shush and send me away
Oh how I hate this time of day
Everyone rushing to be on their way

As the door slams I sit and sigh, I'm all on my own
Can't wait for the time when they all come home
What shall I do while I'm alone?
Can't really use the telephone

Up on the sofa I turn myself round
Guess it's to dreamland that I'm bound
Dreaming of playing and eating my fish
Wake up and stretch and run to my dish

Being alone can be bliss
But three on the clock is a time I never miss
Bang goes the door and in come the kids
Now I just wait for my hug and big kiss

I wait patiently till after they eat
Now it's my time and I'm out of my seat
They play and I chase and tickle their faces
They pet and tickle me in all the right places

I know I'm loved but I know my place
I know I'm loved by the look on their face
My life is sweet and oh so complete
My name is Tom the cat with the black and white feet.

Siobhan Walpole (11)
Our Lady's School

Snow

Snow is joyful,
Not very helpful.
Snow is crystal-white,
I'm going to get frostbite.

Snow is tall,
Sometimes small.
Snow, snow, turns to slush,
Behind that really prickly bush.

Snow is good,
Not like wood.
Snow is great,
Oh I just can't wait.

Snow is fun,
Snow is like an iced bun.
Snow is a pretty sight,
I'm going to have a snowball fight.

Felix Aaron Scollen (11)
Our Lady's School

Summer Sun

S ummer sun, summer fun
U sually the hottest season of the year
M ad, murderous,
M enacing madness!
E veryone loves summer
R eady for the beach yet?

S ummer sun, summer fun
U sually the sun is as hot as Mercury.
N early every sunny day you go out to play.

Megan Roberts (11)
Our Lady's School

Friends

Friends are good,
Friends are great,
Tara is my
Best mate.

Friends are fun,
Friends are cool,
I met most of them
At my school.

Friends are funny,
Friends are fab,
They help me when
Times are bad.

Friends are good,
Friends are great,
Something one should
Appreciate.

Jenny Farrell (11)
Our Lady's School

Celebrations

B irthday, birthday, happy birthday
I love birthdays, they are great
R un and laugh, it's your birthday
T ea is ready, let's eat pizza
'H appy birthday,' everyone sings
D id you have fun at the party?
A t my birthday I have fun
Y ou look great in your new clothes.

Louise Gallagher (11)
Our Lady's School

Sonia's Poem

S un, sun, where have you been?
O ver the hills just like me
N orth, west, south, that's where you've been
I have seen you in places everywhere
A t places you go we see you shining bright all day long.

Sonia Patel (10)
Our Lady's School

Football Kennings

Smelly football boots,
A hair of Smithy's roots.

A new muddy football,
A goal against the wall.

A great goal by Viduka,
Leeds' stunning shooter.

Paul Robinson's corner shoot
And a train that goes hoot, hoot.

You can't just kick it against the wall it's got to be:
Glory, glory Leeds United!

Iona Wilson (10)
Park Spring Primary School

T Rex

T eeth are as big as me

R uns for food
E ats meat from other dinosaurs
eX tra angry!

Macauley Pearson (8)
Park Spring Primary School

Kennings

A skinny boy
A large toy

An annoying child
An infant that goes wild

A big wimp
A cheeky chimp

Some brown hair
But he doesn't care

Some blue eyes
Some whining cries

A messy room
A whistling tune

He's like no other
Because he's my
Brother!

Natalie Farrar (10)
Park Spring Primary School

Mum Kennings

I like to sleep,
and love to eat.

A beautiful smell,
takes care when I'm not well.

She takes a walk,
so she can talk.

A drop of disinfectant,
so I won't get an infection.

Who am I?
. . . Mum!

Sophie Lockwood (11)
Park Spring Primary School

Mum Kennings

A drunken barrel,
An off tune Christmas carol,

An embarrassing hug,
A tiny little bug,

A house cleaner,
As she gets meaner,

A bad cook,
When she runs out of luck,

A loud laugh,
A hot bubble bath,

I like making buns,
Because I'm a loving mum.

Nicole Jade Townend (10)
Park Spring Primary School

Kennings Cat

A fluffy patch of fur
A noisy purr.

A sharp claw
A tiny paw.

Pointy ears
Like a deer's.

A flea collar
That cost a dollar.

Glowing eyes
Baby's cries.

A loud miaow
Do you know what I am?

A cat!

Leah Cowling (11)
Park Spring Primary School

Kennings

A wet nose
a chewed hose.

A furry paw
a sharp claw.

A big bed
a smooth head.

Pointy ears
cute little tears.

A loud bark
when he's in the park.

A chewed log
to make me a dog.

Lauren Bussey (10)
Park Spring Primary School

Tiger

An excellent hunter
with the name Bunter

A friendly purr
some stripy fur

Two staring eyes
like blueberry pies

Perfect paws
with sharp claws

I eat meat
and walk on four feet

Who do you see?
A tiger, that's me.

Alex Skirrow (11)
Park Spring Primary School

Kennings

A graceful climber
As its life is on a timer.

A beast like human
Not as good as Paul Newman.

An echoing whoop
Running from a hunting troop.

Its orange fur
Looks like an ancient sir.

Its feet like hands
As they hang around in a band.

A massive bang

To make me
Orang-utan.

Daniel Reid (11)
Park Spring Primary School

Kennings

A wet nose
a broken hose

a slipper's hole
a snapped bowl

a damp mat
a running cat

a loud bark
a run in the park

a roaring tummy
a cuddle for mummy

a broken cup
to make me a pup.

Sarah-Louise Carr (10)
Park Spring Primary School

Kennings

A magical cook,
A dusty spell book.

A pointy hat,
A brain the size of a newborn cat.

A powerful wand,
As cool as James Bond.

A long cloak,
A spectacular bloke.

A great beard,
A man who is never feared.

As powerful as Harry Potter,
A clever plan plotter.

Who am I?
A wizard.

Sam Gibson (11)
Park Spring Primary School

Kennings

A spoilt brat.
A scum rat.

A nose picker.
A bogie flicker.

A football learner.
A bit of a turner.

A Ninja turtle.
A Pokémon named Squirtle.

A football trainer named Paul.
A cat that's very tall.

A lovely mother
To make an
ugly brother.

Shannon Holmes (10)
Park Spring Primary School

Kennings Dog

A soggy wet nose,
A beautiful baby's pose.

A ragged mat,
A taunted cat.

A broken pot,
I ate the lot.

An energetic pounce,
An enormous bounce.

A chew toy,
A strong boy.

A spilt tea cup,
I must be a rampaging pup.

Michael Lockwood (11)
Park Spring Primary School

Kennings

A brilliant jumper,
With a name called Bumper.

Ten sharp claws,
On fur paws.

Floppy ears,
With dripping tears.

I like to eat,
I never sleep.

I'd like a carrot,
But not a parrot.

Who am I?
I'm a rabbit!

Robert Popple (10)
Park Spring Primary School

Kennings

A sharp claw,
A huge fat boar.

A puppy's tail,
A big bail.

A wet nose,
My chewed-up clothes.

A chewed slipper,
A thrown-up flipper.

A loud bark
That can be heard in the dark.

A huge log,
It must be a dog.

Zoe Lister (10)
Park Spring Primary School

Kennings Whale

The giants of the deep
Who never sleep.

Rough skin,
A rusty metal tin.

Rotten black teeth,
A sharp point of a reef.

A deep black hole,
A red and white pole.

A huge, snappy jaw
And I'm not nice to eat raw.

A very sharp nail
And I'm a whale.

Tyler Brook (11)
Park Spring Primary School

Kennings

I rustle the leaves
Like jingly keys.

I blow the grass
But I soon pass.

I'm ice-cold,
I've been told.

You can't see me anywhere
But I'm still there.

I shiver and shake
And I'm like a snowflake.

Bigger than a sneeze,
More than a breeze

Because I'm the wind.

Toni Bolton (11)
Park Spring Primary School

Kennings Puppy

A cold wet nose,
A cute little pose.

An energetic pounce
And don't care an ounce.

The colour red-wheaten
And doesn't need to sweeten.

Sharp baby teeth
And scares our postman, Keith.

I can never sit still
And chews up the bills.

Flabby, overlapping skin
And I'm never out of the smelly bin.

Who am I? . . . A puppy.

Samantha Thackray (11)
Park Spring Primary School

Kennings Dog

A loud bark,
A nice long walk in the park.

Big, droopy eyes,
I can't tell lies.

A big, juicy bone
And a bowl of beef.

A furry paw,
A sharp claw.

A tin of Bounce,
An extravagant pounce.

If you look in a pet shop's log,
You will find me, a dog.

Zoe McGettigan (10)
Park Spring Primary School

Kennings Dog

I like a walk
So I can talk.

I like to sleep
About humans' feet.

I like any sound
And run around.

A chew toy,
A caring boy.

A lovely pat,
A green hat.

I like a frog
Because I'm a dog.

Hannah Wakefield (11)
Park Spring Primary School

Tiger Kennings

A shiny black stripe
As fast as a motorbike

A huge, sharp claw
A wide open jaw

He senses fear
That he can hear

A loud growl
A hunter on the prowl

A shot of a gun
He's still on the run

Losing speed
As he starts to bleed

The last shot
Hits him right on the spot.

Cruise Lister (11)
Park Spring Primary School

The Aliens

It happened at school I'm sure.
Was it just our class, or maybe more?
Did the aliens want to join in our fun
Or play football outside all day in the sun?
Did the science lesson really take place?
Were the aliens from outer space?

They came for dinner and invaded our school.
We tried our best to keep our cool.
We tucked into hot dogs and fruit-flavoured jellies,
But they wanted our heads to fill their bellies.
They wanted to drink our delicious blood,
But we called in the police before they could.

Ashley Hemingway (10)
Richmond House School

It Happened In My Shed

It happened in my shed I'm sure,
My friend really did have a good cure.
I had a ginormous big spot on my bottom,
The thing that might help is some cotton.
I got rid of the spot on my poor little bot
And threw it in a massive pot.

My bot is now pure
Thanks to the great cure.
My friend was amazed
After he had gazed.
Also my mum and dad
'Cause last time they looked it was bad.

Fraser Shiels (9)
Richmond House School

Squirrels

I have got a secret friend,
Brown and fluffy with a tail as well.
Not a dog. Why don't you guess?
It's a squirrel of course. You should have known!

He eats all the nuts in the acorn tree,
He loves to run and play.
His long, bushy tail lifts as he starts to jump,
He leaps from branch to branch.

Why can't I be a squirrel,
Having so much fun up there,
Eating up all those nuts?
Why can't I have as much happiness up there?

Jessica Lintin (9)
Richmond House School

Skateboarding

It happened in the park I'm sure
When I first realised there was no cure.
Wheels and trucks and decks and speed,
I can't get enough, though sometimes I bleed.
Hours go by and yet I'm never bored,
It's cool when I'm riding my skateboard.

I practise hard to learn new tricks,
Each weekend I get my kicks
Jumping kerbs and curving ramps,
Dodging dogs and concrete lamps.
There's nothing like it for big thrills
But you have to be ready for the spills.

I have a metal grinding rail,
I try and try but still I fail
To slide across its shiny top,
Each time I try I always drop,
So I'll practise hard to get it right
Even if it takes all day and night.

James Wilson (10)
Richmond House School

It Happened On The Bus

It happened on the bus
When travelling to Leeds
That the man next door ate a packet of seeds.
He munched and he chewed and he ate them whole,
Then to my surprise he licked the bowl.
I asked him if I could try some too
He said, 'Check the bag there's a packet for you.'
I tried a few and they tasted like carrots,
I think they're best left for the parrots.

Jennie Stubbs (9)
Richmond House School

It Happened In The Lord Of The Rings I'm Sure

It happened in the ruins of Amon Hen I'm sure
When Boromir thought he saw a wild boar.
Then we ran into the Uruk-Hai
Which was a sight for a sore eye,
But none breached the seeing seat,
It was then the Uruk-Hai knew they were beat.

It happened in the city of Minas Tirith I'm sure
When Gandalf saw ten thousand Orcs plus many more.
Then the Orcs attacked the walls
And the troops of Gondor answered with the strong trebuchet balls.
When the Orcs breached the walls Pippin slew an Orc
With his very own fork.

Henry Cranston (9)
Richmond House School

At The Dentist

It happened at the dentist I'm told,
When I was in the chair I was really bold.
Was he big, was he small?
All I think is that he was tall.
Did he use the drill
Or did he just give me a pill?
Or did he scrape the plaque off my teeth?
Or did he just call me Keith?
Did he just give me a disgusting drink . . .
That was pink?
Did he just say goodbye
And I didn't say anything because I was shy?
I think I went to the reception desk to book an appointment,
I had to have another filling, what a disappointment!

Charlotte Barraclough (10)
Richmond House School

All The Monsters Of The Night!

Ghosts!
Googly, glow in the moonlight.

Big ghosts,
Gigantic grace and a lot of fun.

Small ghosts,
Growing and greets like a blast.

That's not all of the monsters of the night!

Beasts!
Big, bold and not at all old.

Silly beasts,
Silly beasts are as monstrous as a monster truck.

Clever beasts,
Clever, crafty and 2 + 2 is 1 in their case.

That's all the monsters of the night!

Joe Whitehurst (10)
Richmond House School

When I Went To The Zoo

When I went to the zoo
I saw a lion in a cage,
I roared loudly at it
And it roared back with rage!

When I went to the zoo
I saw a vicious rhino behind bars,
It ran straight towards them
And knocked me on the floor,
When I opened my eyes all I saw were stars!

When I went to the zoo
I saw a monkey that was funny,
It told me a joke
And it ran off with my wallet full of money!

Rayhan Ali (10)
Richmond House School

The Writer Of This Poem

(Based on 'The Writer of This Poem' by Roger McGough)

The writer of this poem is . . .
Taller than a skyscraper,
As strong as iron,
As religious as can be.

The writer of this poem is . . .
As sharp as a sword,
As smooth as silk,
As quick as an arrow.

The writer of this poem is . . .
Smarter than a tiger,
As brave as a lion,
As marvellous as can be.

The writer of this poem is
Me.

Malkit Sihra (9)
Richmond House School

My Own Poem

It happened on holiday I'm sure,
I think it was a wolf or something more.
I fell over but I'm not so sure,
Or did I fall down face flat on the floor?
Or did I walk into the door?
It happened on holiday I'm sure.

It happened on holiday I'm sure,
Did it happen on the shore?
I thought that I saw a pirate ship,
On my surfboard I did a flip.
I saw something in the sea, it was a fish,
Its head was shaped like a big dish,
It happened on holiday I'm sure.

Nayab Chaudhry (9)
Richmond House School

The Writer Of This Poem

(Based on 'The Writer of This Poem' by Roger McGough)

The writer of this poem is . . .
As bright as a light,
As right as rain,
As cool as a teacher.

As good as God,
As white as paper,
As happy as a lark,
As sweet as honey.

As funny as a joke,
As warm as wool,
As fit as a fiddle,
As playful as a kitten.

As busy as a bee,
As fresh as a daisy,
As keen as a laptop,
As cute as a bunny.

Charlotte Denison (9)
Richmond House School

The Writer Of This Poem

(Based on 'The Writer of This Poem' by Roger McGough)

The writer of this poem is . . .
As breezy as the wind,
As clever as an elephant,
As helpful as a mother,
As naughty as a boy,
As crisp as a leaf,
As nimble as a footballer,
As bony as a skeleton.

Andrew Coates (10)
Richmond House School

How The Penguin Was Made

For its feet it stole some flippers from a diving instructor,
For its wings it took a paraglider's nylon,
For its beak it took a skewer from the kitchen.

For its feathers it took the blackness of the night
And the sleekness of a fish,
It waddles along due to its loss of flight.

But it can swim so fast it can catch and eat a fish,
For its speed it took a motorboat's engine,
For its supreme agility in the water it took a gymnast's body.

For its disability on land it took a crippled man's legs,
For its ignorance of the cold it took a warm duffel coat,
For its sound it took a screeching violin.

For its surroundings it took the whiteness of a clean sheet,
For its temperature around it, it took the coldness of a freezer,
For its head it took the smoothness of a pebble.

Oliver Penn (10)
Richmond House School

The Mouse

It happened in my room I'm sure,
One or two nights ago, maybe more.
Did someone scream or did they shout
Or was there a ghost flying about?
Then I heard a noisy creak
Or was it really . . . a little squeak?

To my surprise a mouse I could see
Squeaking and squawking and staring at me.
It looked very hungry so I gave it some cheese
And before I could stop it, it jumped on my knees.

Jessica Wetherop (10)
Richmond House School

Silent Sounds Of The Wood

It was so silent that I heard
A squirrel scurry across the open wooded area.

It was so peaceful I heard
The buds of spring opening like a fire crackling.

It was so still I heard
The sun groaning to put out more sunlight.

It was so silent I heard
A bird swooping shyly through the air like an aeroplane.

It was so still that I felt
The wind rush at me like water from a hosepipe.

It was so calm that I sensed
A bird feeding its young quietly.

It was so quiet that I heard
The raindrops pitter-patter on the floor.

Andrew Ward (11)
Richmond House School

The Bedroom Monster

I am sure it all started in my room,
Then I saw it or was that my broom?
I jumped into bed,
'Try not to think about the monster,' my mum said.
Then I turned over, I really did see it,
I saw sharp claws, then I saw it sit.

I heard a tremendous roar,
Please tell me it is not something bad,
Am I dreaming or am I mad?
I decided to turn on my light,
Thinking it was a rat!
Then I saw it, oh it was only my cat.

Rebecca Jackson (9)
Richmond House School

The Balroc

There are older and fouler things than Orcs
In the deeper places of the Earth.

For its face it took
The eyes of the sun,
The horns of a rhino,
The teeth of a shark
And the mouth of a lion.

For its body it took
The strength of an ox,
The wings of an eagle,
The claws of a tiger
And the muscles of a dragon.

For its spirit it took
The power of fire,
The terror of a monster,
The anger of a bull
And the evil of Sauron.

And the Balroc was made.

Barnaby McMahon (11)
Richmond House School

Butterflies

Butterflies are beautiful,
They decorate the world,
They pollinate the flowers,
They flitter-flutter all around like jewels in the sky,
In the air and on the ground,
But it's a shame that they don't live long,
When summer ends they don't stay long.

Charlotte Benstock (9)
Richmond House School

A Silent Poem

It was so silent that I could hear
Hungry ants frantically eating
Like mice scrambling on the floor.

It was so peaceful that I could hear
The hair swishing from side to side
By a passer-by.

It was so still that I could hear
The sun beams
Smiling down on me.

It was so still that I felt
The crisp air
Tickling my face.

It was so calm that I sensed
The grass swaying
To the rhythm of the wind.

It was so quiet that I heard
The raindrops splashing on the ground
Like pebbles in a pond.

Oliver Packman (10)
Richmond House School

Our Cat Max

Our cat Max was black all over,
But when we moved house
He got run over.
We buried him in the garden
And cried and cried some tears,
But we know we'll think of him
For many, many years.

Nicholas Winn (7)
Richmond House School

Doom!

It happened at the beach I know,
I was ready for The Simpsons show!
Was it a power cut? Was it a war?
I saw a ghost really I'm sure.
What was it that made the TV go black?
I was so scared, I hid in my anorak!

I'm positive it started in my brother's bedroom,
I heard the evil voice of doom!
Was it my bro? Was it a ghost?
Suddenly I was hit by a piece of toast.
Sadly I don't know any more,
Because I ran out and slammed the door!

It happened in space, I'm sure,
There was a bump and a rumble at the door.
Was it aliens? Was it a comet?
The captain just sat there playing Bop It!
It was scary I had to go,
I couldn't miss The Simpsons show!

Eleanor Browne (9)
Richmond House School

When I Was In The Stables

When I was in the stables
I saw lots of horses,
I mounted one of the ponies
And did some big courses.

When I was in the stables
My horse gave me a cuddle,
It was a wet day
And my horse stepped in a big puddle.

Sherriden Rastegar (9)
Richmond House School

When I Was In Africa

When I was in Africa
There was an elephant who was rather cute,
I climbed up for a ride,
She was not really minute!

When I was in Africa
I saw a giraffe that was red and black,
It was rather large,
I climbed up on its back!

When I was in Africa
I saw a lovely monkey,
He had a funny hairstyle,
I thought it was really funky!

Molly Hayward (9)
Richmond House School

It Was On A Submarine

It was on a submarine, I think,
Was it afloat or was it about to sink?
Was it called Ann or was it Sue
Or was it coloured turquoise-blue?
Was I asleep
Or did I hear the sinking beep?

I saw the captain strolling and singing a song,
He said it was running smoothly along.
I was sure he was wrong, I believed,
But still I was relieved,
I looked out the window and saw a colour which was brill,
Then I realised it was krill.

Mike Wren-Kirkham (9)
Richmond House School

My Teeth

My teeth are sparkling white,
I look at other people's teeth, they give me a fright!
Their teeth are practically green,
Those people are so obscene and mean!

I love my teeth, they're a wonderful thing,
When I look in the mirror, they almost ping!
I can't wait to be a bride and walk down the aisle,
What a husband *loves* is a wonderful smile.

Hannah Donkin (9)
Richmond House School

My Secret Friend

Bushy tail it does have,
But not a fox I say.
Charming in its woodland outback,
Swiftly soaring through the trees.
Maybe it was here,
Maybe it was there.
But really it is so speedy,
You would never have known it was there.

Katie Parsloe (8)
Richmond House School

The Two Ladies

It happened next to my door, ça s'est passé,
There were two ladies, j'y ai pensé.
Were they singing or did they dance?
Was it in France?
Did they hit me with an arc
Or were they going to the parc?

Juliette Izard (9)
Richmond House School

Jelly On A Plate

When Kelly came for tea
We had jelly for her and me,
Big as a mound and round as a pound.

'Jelly on a plate
Jelly on a plate
Wibble, wobble
Wibble, wobble
Jelly on a plate.'

When Kelly came for tea
We had jelly for her and me,
Slippery as a slope and gooey as soap.

'Jelly on a plate
Jelly on a plate
Wibble, wobble
Wibble, wobble
Jelly on a plate.'

When Kelly came for tea
We had jelly for her and me,
Sweet as a sugar beet and as red as red can be.

'Jelly on a plate
Jelly on a plate
Wibble, wobble
Wibble, wobble
Jelly
          Off
               The
                    Plate.'

Daisy Lee (8)
Richmond House School

The Moon

There is a big thing
Up in the sky at night.
What is it? I ask myself.
It was white and looked as if
It was a big, giant eye
Shining in the midnight sky.

There was a man who lived
Up high in the sky.
He lived on the moon.
He sat up on the moon at night
And had a look.
What was in his sight?

Each and every single day
A star flew past
And knocked him off the moon quite fast!
He spun and spun until he went dizzy
And into a star he crashed.
The star led him back to the moon.

Safely back at home again,
That's the man on the moon!

Jessica Lloyd (7)
Richmond House School

Cricket

In cricket you get a wicket,
You can have a four or a six,
Unless you hit the sticks.
If you are the winner you
Can head straight to dinner.
One match could take an hour or a day,
After the game you can go away.

Adam Bowie (7)
Richmond House School

My Sister Is A Pain

My big sister is such a pain,
She is always likely to complain.
She moans and moans whatever I do,
Even if I put a spider in her shoe.

Always screaming and shouting,
Forever going on an outing.
But that's not fair on me,
I wish she could get stung by a bee.

She looks slimy and yucky,
Her boyfriend calls her Ducky.
Her singing is really so bad,
It drives me completely mad,
Even though I'm a little lad.

She could make a baby cry
Just looking it in the eye.
My big sister is such a pain,
I'm never going to speak to her again.

Alex Shaw (7)
Richmond House School

Phones, Great Phones

A big ringer,
A tremendous hanger,
A button presser,
An electricity user,
A wire attacker,
A big microphone,
A phone line traveller,
An answer phone machine,
A world connector,
A phone time stalker.

John Brady (9)
Richmond House School

Moon Man

The moon man is a very desperate man,
He is on a mission to find some aliens,
He has to find a rocket
To fly him to planet Zob,
He also has a dog,
Who happens to be called Mog.

Now they're on planet Zob
It's not what they thought,
There are no aliens,
There's nothing there but . . .
Frogs!

Fahad Durrani (7)
Richmond House School

The Butterfly

A butterfly is very shy,
A butterfly is a kind of guy
Who travels up so high.
My little brother is as lovely as a pie
But I sigh.
He has to die,
Oh my poor little butterfly.

George Barker (8)
Richmond House School

Candle

Candle, candle burning flame,
Candle, candle light again.
Candle, candle in the dark,
Candle, candle such a heart.

Elliot Pawley (8)
Richmond House School

A Lion!

The lion began,
It took the yellow of the sun.
It stole the hair from a model
For its mane.

For its fur coat
It took the gleam of the sunflower
And the softness of springy hair,
To increase the heat of the lion.

To help it hunt
It took the sharpness of a knife,
The steadiness of a gymnast
To make its claws.

To make its tail
It took the body of a snake,
The smoothness of velvet
And the lion was made.

Julia Shaw (10)
Richmond House School

Tennis

Tennis is a great game,
Some people think it's lame.
It is a brilliant sport
That is played on a court.
You play with a racquet and a ball,
You have the advantage if you're tall.
You can play a smash or a spinner,
You always hope that you're the winner.
Even if you just don't win
Another game will soon begin.

Alex Orbaum (7)
Richmond House School

One Naughty Nightingale

One naughty nightingale nagging at my knees.
Two tottering tigers thrashing around the trees.

Three trampling termites toppling around my feet.
Four flopping falcons flying at a hundred feet.

Five fish flinging stones at each other.
Six baby snakes biting at their mother.

Seven sobbing scorpions squashing the sand.
Eight elongated elephants crushing everything but my hand.

Nine nasty newts biting at my heels.
Ten ticking terrapins knocking at the eels.

Joe Ingham (11)
Richmond House School

Will

I have a dog and his name is Will,
He lives with me at Hicklam Mill,
Every morning we have a walk,
After that we have a talk.

I have a dog and his name is Will,
He lives with me at Hicklam Mill,
We have such fun, we splash in the puddles,
After that we have lots of cuddles.

Elizabeth Hey (7)
Richmond House School

My Dogs

My dad took my dogs to the park,
They had to get home before dark.
My dogs went barking mad,
Then went over and bit my dad!

Annie Marshall (7)
Richmond House School

How The Giraffe Was Made

How the giraffe was made,
It took the tall trees
And the massive mountains
For its neck.

For its legs
It took the poles from a rugby pitch,
It took the sticks from a wood
And the length of the sun.

For its ears
It took the flapping of wings,
It took the straightness of a ruler.

For the colours it took
The spots from a tiger,
The yellow of a banana
And the black from a panther.

For the tail it took
The length of a snake,
It took the felt from a coat
And the feel of string.

Elliott Habgood (10)
Richmond House School

Castles

Castles were built long ago,
Everyone in them had to be bold,
If they weren't bold they couldn't fight,
But the castle would keep them safe at night.

Hugo Calder (7)
Richmond House School

The Wind's Song

It was so quiet I heard
Creeping ants steady footfalls
On the grass outside.

It was so silent that I heard
The whisper
An endless song . . .

It was so still that I heard
The breeze going through the trees,
Rustling the leaves.

It was so peaceful I heard
The window drying,
After a stormy night.

It was so silent that I heard
The sun breathing heavily
In boredom.

It was so calm that I sensed
The grass listening to the
Song of silence.

It was so quiet that I heard
The earth listening to the orchestra of the trees,
Like a giant breathing softly.

Oliver Iles (10)
Richmond House School

Uncle Harry Back From War

Uncle Harry back from war,
Uncle Harry have a drink,
Uncle Harry do you want it from the sink?
Uncle Harry back from war,
Uncle Harry wave your flag,
Uncle Harry let's play tag,
Uncle Harry back from war.

James Donahue (7)
Richmond House School

Football Is Great

F ootball is my favourite game
O liver Wilson is my name
O le Gunnar Solskjaer, Man U's striker
T hierry Henry, Arsenal's French ace
B eckham is my all time hero
A lways up and down scoring great goals
L eeds United is my favourite team
L asher Lorimer had the hottest shot.

I only wish he was still playing
S eventy miles an hour strikes on goal.

G oals galore are what we need
R elegation fears will disappear
E lland Road's the only place for us
A place in their team is my dream
T o score a goal and hear fans scream.

Oliver Wilson (8)
Richmond House School

My Life

My life is like a squirrel's life
Whirling up a tree,
I race around
And jump and play
With everything I see.

I climb along a climbing frame
Looking for a leaf,
When then I spot an oak tree
And an acorn underneath.

Toby Ellison-Scott (7)
Richmond House School

How The Shark Was Made

For the shape
He took the streamlined shape of a Ferrari,
The tail of a fighter jet
And the flatness of water.

For the jaws
He took the sharpness of a diamond-edged knife.
He took the power of hydraulic pistons
And he took the strength of a steel bar.

For the colour
He took the greyness of stone,
The darkness of space
And the flatness of marble.

For the instinct
He took the aggressiveness of a carnivorous dinosaur,
The scent of a bloodhound
And the brain of a dolphin.

For the speed
He took the fastness of a bolt of lightning,
The acceleration of a roller coaster
And the G-force of a spaceship.

James Parsloe (11)
Richmond House School

A Dolly Called Polly

There once was a dolly
And her name was Polly.
She was very jolly
And she had a sister called Holly.
One day they went to the park
And saw their friend Mark.
He was playing darts
With his friend Bart
Who was very smart
And lived in a cart.

Holly Wilson (7)
Richmond House School

The Shark

For its skin it took
The sharp roughness of untouched sandpaper,
The individuality of each sharp granule of its skin
Like the grains of sand on the beach.

For its teeth it took
The sharp hardness of ice,
Like many spear points tearing into flesh.

For its eyes it took
The blackness of a large beetle,
The darting movements of a frantic spider.

For its speed it took
The speed of a large motorboat skimming across
The smooth, cool surface of an undisturbed water,
The power of an Aston Martin.

For its great power it took
The strength of an entire army fighting in the sea,
The great hit of a guided missile.

Alex Browne (10)
Richmond House School

One Gibbering Gibbon

One gibbering gibbon grabbing onto me,
Two turquoise turtles swimming in the sea.
Three tight tigers tickling me torturingly,
Four dirty dinosaurs biting a tree.
Five flying foxes zooming over me,
Six slow sloths sleeping in a tree.
Seven dim dodos jumping off a tree,
Eight eating elephants trumpeting at the flea.
Nine nosy nightingales walking away from Lee,
Ten tipsy terrapins lying on my knee.

Ben Perren (10)
Richmond House School

The Silent Sounds Of The Park

It was so silent in the park that I heard
The thin roots of grass
Extend themselves through the soil.

It was so quiet in the park that I heard
The beautiful white moon
Rising above the trees.

It was so peaceful in the park that I heard
The thoughts of a worm
Digging deep below me.

It was so still in the park that I heard
A bird nestling
High up in the trees.

It was so calm in the park that I heard
The dying sounds
Of an old oak.

It was so quiet in the park that I heard
The stars whisper
About the beauty of the Earth.

It was so still in the park that I heard
The blink of an eye
Of a park keeper.

It was so calm in the park that I heard
The craving crocus
Closing its bright petal.

It was so silent in the park that I heard
Dust travelling over
The ground in lovely clouds.

Oliver Dixon (11)
Richmond House School

A Poem To Be Read Silently

It was so silent that I heard
The moon crying
Like the baby from next door.

It was so peaceful that I heard
A bird's wing flap
Like a cat flap flapping.

It was so still that I heard
The floorboards creaking
Like a mouse squeaking.

It was so silent that I heard
The bark of a tree
Talking to its leaves
Like a mum to its baby.

It was so still that I could hear
My mother's voice reading a story
Like an echo in a tunnel.

It was so still that I could hear
The buzzing of the computer
Like a bee in its hive.

It was so quiet that I heard
Ants scurrying over my
Squeaking floorboards
Like elephants over the desert floor.

Ben Sweeting (10)
Richmond House School

Morning Has Broken, No One Can Fix It

I want to get up and play with my toys,
I must go to school but there are too many boys,
Perhaps I'll stay here because they make too much
Noise.

Natalie Brykalski (8)
Richmond House School

Silence Surrounds Us

The silence surrounded me,
I heard the glowing moon sail across the starry sky
Like a boat moving across the sea.

Soothing sounds ripple across the sparkling, darkening sea.

The quietness surrounded me, I heard the trees chatter
Motionless in my surroundings.

Lulling noises eased in and out of the swaying green luscious grass.

The calmness surrounded me, I heard the flowers
Having a tea party and dancing.

Redeeming sounds echoed all around my straining ear.

The stillness surrounded me, I heard symmetrical butterfly
Wings flutter like thunder crashing together.

Noises, sounds and calmness surrounded me.

Emma Moran (11)
Richmond House School

One Wonderful Wombat

One wonderful wombat wriggling up a tree.
Two terrifying tigers hunting for their tea.

Three thin thrushes thrashing things around.
Four fabulous flies forgetting to make a sound.

Five funny foals jumping in the stable.
Six singing songbirds singing all they're able.

Seven smelly skunks stinking out the room.
Eight eager elephants hoping to eat soon.

Nine naughty nightingales keeping all awake.
Ten tiny turtles swimming in the lake.

Celia Marker (10)
Richmond House School

When I Look In The Zoo I See . . .

When I look in the zoo I see . . .
A monkey climbing a great big tree.

I see birds flying all around,
A tiger making a ferocious sound.

I see a rhino with a great big horn,
A baby cub not long born.

I see an elephant with his long, long trunk,
But next to his mum he looks like he's shrunk.

I see lions with their great big jaws
And a Siamese cat licking his paws.

I see a crocodile showing his shiny teeth
While the others are ripping up some juicy beef.

I see a donkey eating from a bunch of weed
And chimps jumping on their furry feet.

I see a skunk with a really bad smell,
What he'd eaten I couldn't tell.

The zoo is closing,
The monkeys are posing.

The animals are off to sleep.

James Deaves (11)
Ryecroft Primary School

A Funky Limerick

There was a person called Dash
Who had very little cash
So he got himself a job
And changed his name to Bob
So when he went home he made some mash.

Daniel Burdon (11)
Ryecroft Primary School

Monkbaderger

The monkbaderger has the body of a tiger
And the head of a spider,
A bat's wings, a monkey's tail and feet,
Everybody knows it likes meat.

This magnificent creature locked away,
People come to see him every day,
He likes to fly
Up in the sky,
Some day people will pay
To see this creature locked away.

Rebecca Jackson (10)
Ryecroft Primary School

There Was A Young Girl From Mauritius

There was a young girl from Mauritius
Who said that last sandwich was delicious
But next time you make it
Will you make it by baking it
Coz that ham in the middle looks suspicious.

Mary Hoop (11)
Ryecroft Primary School

The Licking Chicken

There was a very young chicken
Who was always obsessed with licking
She went into town
And met a silly old clown
Then went off strawberry picking.

Sean McCleary (11)
Ryecroft Primary School

Wanted

The sneaker's a freak,
The sneaker's a geek.
He comes at night,
He doesn't like the light.
He smells like a welly,
He has a big belly.
He's getting weaker and weaker,
Has anyone seen the sneaker?

Jodie Stephenson (11)
Ryecroft Primary School

The School Run!

Alarm ringing,
Early mornings,
Tired eyes,
Striding out,
Traffic flowing,
Stop, look, listen,
Say bye to Mum,
School starting.

School's out,
Hustle and bustle,
Rushing and shoving,
Gossiping mums,
Tired children
Waiting at the bus stop,
Traffic passing,
Bus is coming,
Tickets please,
It's our stop.

Jade Barlow (11)
St Peter's CE Primary School

I Love The Sea

The whirlpools twirl and twist,
Underneath the fog and mist.
There is a sea sapphire-blue,
Here for me, here for you.
The sea is calm, the sea is clear,
Rolling waves you will hear.
Sea horses echo underneath,
The sand and the coral reef.
Shoals of fish swim over there,
Right into the shark's lair.
The fish try to swim down low,
But the shark gets them all in one go.
Sea, shells and rocks are beautiful things,
Fishes' gills like butterflies' wings.
Jellyfish glow like stars in the sky,
Octopuses' tentacles whooshing by.
Eels curl, eels flash,
Dolphins glide, dolphins splash.
There is a sea sapphire-blue,
Here for me, here for you.

Abigail Forrester (11)
St Peter's CE Primary School

The Future

I'm only ten now but I still look to the future,
I sometimes think I might need a tutor.

I've got all my life in front of me,
High school will be coming soon, that will be good for me.

I'm a bit scared but I'll pull through,
It's music class really, I don't think I can come in on the right cue.

Then it's the college years, what's going on?
Do I really want to go there? I might have to make a song.

Oh no, what have I done, I'm going to university,
It's in London in the middle of the city.

It's the husband now,
I hope we don't have another row.

Now here's the kids, they're driving me mad,
Can't they go off and annoy their dad.

Well no need to worry, thank God I'm still ten,
I don't need to think about kids or men.

I think it's time to put down my pen.

Tshanna Adams (10)
St Peter's CE Primary School

Worries

Worry, worry, worry, worry,
Worry, worry, worry, worry,
Have you got a worry
Messing up your head?
Do you feel in a flurry?
Do you wish you were dead?

Worry, worry, worry, worry,
Worry, worry, worry, worry,
Do you have a secret fear?
Do you hate the way you look?
Do you shed a secret tear?
Seek an answer from a book?

Worry, worry, worry, worry,
Worry, worry, worry, worry,
Can't find a solution?
Can't get to sleep at night?
Do you worry about pollution,
Starving people, men that fight?

Worry, worry, worry, worry,
Worry, worry, worry, worry,
Do your worries make you blush?
Are you scared to spit it out?
Do you blurt it out in a rush?
Are you cast down in doubt?

Worry, worry, worry, worry,
Worry, worry, worry, worry,
Your friends will show they care
With comments frank but fond,
It will help us all to share
And Miss White will wave her wand
To stop you going . . .
Worry, worry, worry, worry,
Worry, worry, worry, worry,
        Worry!

Salomey Adjei-Doku (9)
St Peter's CE Primary School

My Family

My sister Emma
always causes a dilemma.

My sister Jade
looks like a spade.

My sister Katie
is a rotten tatie.

My mum Julie
floats like a ghoulie.

My mum's boyfriend Pete
loves to eat.

My grandma Ruth
is like a tooth.

My grandad Dave
lives in a cave.

My auntie Heather
likes to predict the weather.

My auntie Helen
loves to eat melon.

My auntie Gail
looks like a whale.

My uncle Brian
snores like a lion.

My cousin Shane
is a pain.

My cousin Ben
sleeps in a den.

My cousin Gary
is as lanky as Larry.

My cousin Michelle
loves ringing her bell.

Lisa Adams (7)
St Peter's CE Primary School

The Four Seasons

S pring is a beautiful season,
P ouncing lambs play in fields,
R ed rosebuds start to bloom,
I ndigo crocuses cover the ground,
N ew bird nests are built,
G ales of winter are gone.

S ummer is extremely hot,
U mbrellas for shade are needed,
M ore sun than you could imagine,
M usical ice cream vans everywhere,
E very plant is in full bloom,
R ich colours flood each garden.

A ll the trees are dying,
U nder the trees all of the leaves lay,
T hrush and its fellow birds migrate,
U nderneath the dull sky animals start to hibernate,
M ice collect food ready to store,
N asty weather is on its way.

W inter months are very cold,
I cicles hang from some people's roofs,
N umb fingers and toes people get,
T all trees stand empty and bare,
E very house is kept warm and cosy,
R ounding off the year the last season is winter.

Stephanie Finch (11)
St Peter's CE Primary School

A Better Place

I wish the world was a better place
To sit and relax and watch my pace,
But it will be better if it's holy,
But you have to practise really slowly.

I wish the world were really caring
But at least it can be a little sharing.
My friends, my family, my cousins too
They're really kind, I think they'll do.

I wish the world was helpful
And also really cheerful.
No pain, no harm, no sadness too,
It makes me cry, what about you?

But one thing I know
A little love, a little kindness
Will go a long way
To make our world a better place.

Achese Hector-Goma (7)
St Peter's CE Primary School

If You Want To See A Lion

(Based on 'If You Want To See An Alligator')

If you want to see a lion
You must go down to the sticky, roasty grassland.

I know a lion
Who's living down there,
He's mean, he's fierce, he's horrible, he's a killer.

Yes, if you really want to see a lion
You must go down to the sticky, roasty grassland.

Go down and quietly go to the grassland
And say, 'Lion Papa, Lion Papa, Lion Papaaaaaaaa.'

And out of nowhere he comes
But *run fast or you'll be lunch.*

Andrew Adjei-Doku (8)
St Peter's CE Primary School

My School

My school is a fun place to be,
Its name's St Peter's on Cromwell Street.
It's got 7 classrooms and a hall too,
A library, an office, also a computer room.

It's full of teachers you'd love to see,
Lots of cheerful children you'd like to meet.
The teachers are very clever and bold,
The children are as good as gold.

We're provided with toys to play with outside,
Os and Xs, dominoes, even giant 4 in a line.
My school is a fair one, they care for us so much
Cos they know we're such a special bunch.

So next time you're in the city of Leeds,
Take a look at St Peter's on Cromwell Street.
Our school motto is, *'we care'*,
And we have such a joyful 6 hours while we're there!

Athene-Nanette Idiabor-Moses (10)
St Peter's CE Primary School

Snowflake

Snowflake, watch them falling by,
The snow is coming from the sky.
The sky wind blows the snow
So they fly away.

So much snow pours on my roof,
I'll huff and puff and blow the snow down.
Everyone goes outside with amazement.

Now the sun is shining
It's time to let the snow go!
The snow is melting very, very slowly,
Now wait for next year,
Till it will snow for a surprise.

Anujesupo Alabi (9)
St Peter's CE Primary School

Growing Up

This is how a normal life may come around,
As a small child
I sat there and smiled,
Wondered what will become of me,
In my future years.

Now my age is ten,
I'm working hard in school,
So I don't end up a fool!

Getting older, getting bolder.
Thirteen, I am becoming a teenager.
Mum says I'll be awful, she'll put on a wager.

Getting taller like my cousin Paula,
Sixteen, sweet and happy,
Passed all my exams, what a big feat.

I'm so grown up, no longer a pup.
Eighteen, away at college, to study further.
Missing home,
Keep meaning to phone.

It's been hard work, but I won't shirk.
Twenty-one, having lots of fun,
Time to have a year in the sun!

We'll miss a few, forty is where we'll skip to!
Forty, life begins here so they say!
Life's going a really good way.
House and a job and a husband too,
Kids growing the way they do!

Oh no! It's the day I feared,
I'm feeling weird!
Twilight years are here.
The years have gone by, so much to show,
Where did the time go?

But luckily I'm only ten, don't need to worry,
There's no need to hurry!

Adele Elizabeth Johnson (10)
St Peter's CE Primary School

My Family

Some people have large families,
Some people have small.
Mine is medium and I think that's best of all.

First there's my dad,
He likes fishing and rugby,
Worst of all he just knows how to bug me.

Then there's my mum,
She likes karaoke singing,
She really knows how to get a party swinging.

Next there's my brother,
I wouldn't swap him for any other,
We fight and we tease
Then we get told off by our mother.

Then there's me the youngest of all,
When I was young my mum said all I did was bawl.
Look at me now, 11 years old, guess what! I still don't
Do as I'm told.

Becky Robinson (11)
St Peter's CE Primary School

Dolphins

D olphins have fun every single day,
O ceans are wide for dolphins to play,
L earning to dive and to flip their fin,
P ointing to the ocean while they spin,
H appy dolphins sing a song,
 I n the ocean all day long,
N ear the horizon as we can see,
S wimming along proud and free.

Kirsty Heyes (10)
St Peter's CE Primary School

Human Beings

Many human beings are caring,
But some are not.
Many human beings are loving,
But some are not.
Many human beings are friendly,
But some are not.
Many human beings are lonely,
But many are *not!*

Some human beings are bullies,
Lots are not.
Some human beings are hurtful,
But many are not.
Some human beings are nasty,
But many are not.
Some humans don't care for others,
But lots and lots *do!*

Ben Mowbray (10)
St Peter's CE Primary School

There Was A Police Lady Called Kate

There was a police lady called Kate
Who always would arrive very late,
She was never on time
At the scene of the crime,
That careless police lady called Kate.

Sinead Flanagan (11)
St Peter's CE Primary School

Let There Be Peace In The World

Let there be peace on Earth,
No bombing and people running.

Let there be peace on Earth,
Me, Mum and Dad playing in the field
And no more TV dinner meals.

Let there be peace on Earth,
No more news of people dying
And relatives crying.

Let there be peace on Earth,
When Mum stops crying
And Dad stops lying.

Let there be peace on Earth,
No more moving from one place to another
And no more kids living without their mother.

When there is peace in the world
The world will be a better place.

Iberedem Udoh (10)
St Peter's CE Primary School

Friends

We should all be friends,
We should care and lend.
It shouldn't matter what colour,
We should all play with each other.
If you have friends
Your lovely heart will mend.

                        That's why
                        You need
                        Your friends.

Jake Meredith (8)
St Peter's CE Primary School

Birthdays

Birthdays, birthdays,
It's such fun.
Birthdays, birthdays
For everyone!
Birthdays, birthdays,
Mum's going to bake.
Birthdays, birthdays,
A great big cake.
Birthdays, birthdays,
Lots of new toys.
Birthdays, birthdays
For girls and boys.
Birthdays, birthdays
I can't wait.
Birthdays, birthdays
Are really *great!*

Chelsea Aveyard (8)
St Peter's CE Primary School

My Teacher Is A Monster

Who's that stomping round the room
With a wooden spoon
Bursting with anger?
Her piercing eyes, her sharp fingers
And her spiky hair,
No one dare move or make a sound
While my teacher is around.

John Gibson (9)
Swillington Primary School

The Magic Box

(Based on 'Magic Box' by Kit Wright)

I will put in my box . . .
The first flower to bloom in spring,
The smell of bacon as my dad makes the breakfast,
The crunch of leaves as I walk in the autumn.

I will put in my box . . .
The feel when you dive in a swimming pool,
The taste of waffles when you're at the seaside,
The noise of bubble wrap when you pop it.

I will put in my box . . .
The noise of a hooting owl in the night,
The sigh of a whale,
A baby's first laugh.

My box is silver with a gold pattern on the lid.

Rachel Curtis (9)
Swillington Primary School

A Peaceful Night

The night is peaceful,
Not a person in sight,
Only the stars and the moon bring light,
Not a bird flies in the sky,
The clouds all hidden way up high,
Eyes start to close and off people doze,
People's dreams bring smiles and fright,
Don't shout, whisper goodnight.

Lauren Cheesbrough (9)
Swillington Primary School

Snow

S now, snow where do you go?
    Please tell me because I don't know.
N ight falls, snow comes,
    Spreads all over the world.
O h snow, oh snow, where do you come from?
    Please tell me because I want to know.
W hite snow is in my garden,
    Spreads the plants into a waterfall.

Lois Jones (8)
Swillington Primary School

Animals

Michael the monkey munches meat on Mars.
Cracker the crocodile likes cracking cracks in Canada.
Freddy the fly likes finding feathers in France.
Sally the seal likes stealing scissors in Stanley.
Garry the giraffe likes getting papers in Galveston.
Steve the spider spits in Spain.
Luke the lion likes lollies in Luxembourg.

Hannah Carmichael (8)
Swillington Primary School

Snake

Slimy snakes slither and slide.
Luke the lion likes licking lollies.
Charlotte the chocolate bar cooks cookies.
Danny donkey likes to dive.
Ray the rhino rides his bike.

Luke Monks-Palmer (8)
Swillington Primary School

At The Beach

The beach has golden sand and bright sunshine
And the cool, refreshing sea.

B est fish and chips definitely come from the seaside,
E xtremely soft towels rubbing against your skin after
    you've been in the salty sea.
A n ice cream melting in your hand.
C unning seagulls making prints in the sand.
H ome again, but feeling tired, as you've had lots of fun.

That's why for a brilliant time
Beaches are definitely my no 1!

Emma Wallace (9)
Swillington Primary School

Animals

Tigger the tiny toad plays tennis in Turkey.
Sammy the smelly snake likes swimming in Swillington.
Billy the big bird likes bouncing in Blackpool.
Lily the loud lion likes lollies in Liverpool.
Betty the beautiful bee likes bugs in Belgium.

Jade Linley (8)
Swillington Primary School

The Stormy Night

One normal day but a stormy night,
A ghost jumped out and gave me a fright,
I was all alone in a scary wood,
I ran away from a vampire as fast as I could.
Now you know about this stormy night,
You know which places give you a fright.

Chloe Hanlon (9)
Swillington Primary School

Clever Animals From Around The World

Timmy the tidy tiger
teaches tricks in Turkey.

Ryan the revolting rhino
reads in Russia.

Dimmy the delightful dolphin
dances in Denmark.

Charlie the cheerful cheetah
is careful with craft in Canada.

Hannah the horrible hippo
does handstands on holiday in Hawaii.

Paige the patient panda
plays with people in Pakistan.

Sarah the smiley snake
is surrounded by sunflowers in Switzerland.

Awesome animals are in alliteration
around the atlas.

Charlotte Wallis (8)
Swillington Primary School

Animal Alliteration

Paige the pretty polar bear politely plays peek-a-boo,
Craig the crocodile crossly crunches creamy crackers,
Tina the tortoise's tears trickle down her tired, tearful face,
Brogan the bull softly blows blue bubbles,
Jolly Josie joyfully jumps and sings Jingle Bells,
Dancing Daisy dizzily dances in darkness with her dressing gown on,
Leo the lion lies soundly asleep in the long grass.
    As the sun falls and the day ends,
    There's no sound, just peace and quiet.

Emily Waldron (8)
Swillington Primary School

The Romantic Poem

V iolins play romantically,
A day when everyone loves,
L ovely couples eat love heart chocolates,
E ventually peace and rest,
N ow everything is beautiful,
T wo of everything,
I give my parents a hug and a kiss,
N ow red roses are given,
E veryone is joyful,
S ummer is on its way. *Yippee!*

Brogan Louise Nugent (8)
Swillington Primary School

The Lovely Poem

V alentines
A dore
L over
E verlasting
N ice
T hankful
I n love
N ever-ending
E verything is love
S miles.

Rosie Whelan (9)
Swillington Primary School

DIY

D o the drilling now
I t makes your house look better
Y ou can do anything if you DIY.

Luke Smith (9)
Swillington Primary School

Colour Poem

White is like the snow,
Falling from the winter sky,
A polar bear in the frost,
The colour of a stork walking by.

Red is the lipstick upon my mother's lips,
Is Mars staying put in space,
The blood from an injury,
The rosy red cheeks on my face.

Yellow are the feathers on a canary,
The colour of the rising sun,
The sign of summer,
Or the melting ice cream rolling off your tongue.

Green are the reeds,
Lying by a river bank,
The salty seaweed,
Or the leftovers in a fish tank.

Purple is a felt tip,
Drawing on A4,
The colour of a pansy,
Rising from the floor.

Black is a shadow,
Wandering into the night,
The colour of wet soil,
An ant scurrying from the sunlight.

Gold is the colour of a pirate's destiny,
The pound in my coat pocket,
The colour of an eagle,
The colour of my broken locket.

Charlotte Gibson (10)
Swillington Primary School

Birds

B irds are lovely
I like birds
R obin redbreasts are the best
D ucks quacking
S parrows are nice.

Hugh-Grant Babbage (8)
Swillington Primary School

In The Jungle

Sam the snake is smashing at slithering silently,
Tina the tiger is tremendous at tiptoeing,
Peter the parrot punches a penny,
Ellie the elephant enjoys enormous elephants.

Holly McManus (8)
Swillington Primary School

There Was A Boy In My Class

There was a boy in my class
Who broke a very big glass,
He fell on the floor,
Banged his head on the door
And rolled about on the grass.

Christian Hughes (8)
Swinnow Primary School

The Foolish Girl Who Dressed Cool

There was a young girl who was foolish
She came to school dressed coolish,
She wore a leather jacket
And had a sweet rabbit
But her thoughts were always ghoulish.

Stacey Louise Sharp (7)
Swinnow Primary School

In My Class

There was an ugly girl in my class
She always wore a funny mask
She was not very bright
But she was sometimes right
And tumbled onto the green grass.

Emma Urwin (8)
Swinnow Primary School

There Was A Girl In My Class

There was a girl in my class
Who wore a glorious mask.
Came to school dressed cool,
People called her a fool,
So she went and hid in the grass.

Stacey Wade (8)
Swinnow Primary School

The Little Girl

There was a little girl in my class,
She nearly broke my glass,
I went into the hall,
I started to fall,
I ran back to the class very fast.

Natasha Hardisty (8)
Swinnow Primary School

My Mum's Story Haiku

My mum is so kind
We go out on a warm day
I love my mum lots.

Ashleigh Abbott (10)
Swinnow Primary School

The Foolish Teacher

There was a teacher who was a fool
She wasn't very popular in school
She had slimy hair
She wasn't very fair
She came back to school as a mule.

Charlotte Bell (7)
Swinnow Primary School

At School

There was a boy who was cool
And came to school as a fool
He was so bad
It made him sad
So he turned himself into a mule.

Callum Riley (8)
Swinnow Primary School

Jim's Day

There was a boy called Jim
Who was very, very slim
He was a fool
In the swimming pool
Who always came out with a grin.

Lloyd Reilly (8)
Swinnow Primary School

Cat's Haiku

Purring through the night
She wakes me up in my bed
My cat is my friend.

Rebekah Richardson (10)
Swinnow Primary School

The Foolish Boy

There was a little boy in school
Who sat on a rusty stool
He tripped on the wall
And felt nothing at all
He felt such a foolish fool.

Natasha Todd (8)
Swinnow Primary School

The Cool Person

There was a girl in my school,
She was ever so cool,
The kids loved her,
The cats did purr,
Oh dear, she fell in the pool.

Jade Harsley (8)
Swinnow Primary School

The New Teacher In School

There was a new teacher in school
She made the children act cool
She took them to the zoo
They got stuck in a queue
So they went to the swimming pool.

Thomas Barnes (7)
Swinnow Primary School

Majorettes Haiku

Twiddling my baton,
Competition time again.
Marching down the lane.

Tamra Morton (9)
Swinnow Primary School

The Sick Boy

There was a boy who was ill
The teacher gave him a pill
He felt really sick
He did a big kick
The teacher said, 'Are you ill still?'

Ewan Dockerty (7)
Swinnow Primary School

New Boy

There was a new boy in class
Who wore a funny mask
Everyone thought he was fun
He gave them a bun
Then he saw a man with a tash.

Shola Morton (7)
Swinnow Primary School

A Foolish Boy

There was a boy who was a fool
But he also dressed to be cool
Was in the school team
He wanted to meet the Queen
At the thought he began to drool.

Adam Teggart (8)
Swinnow Primary School

The Lord Of The Rings Haiku

The Lord of the Rings
Frodo destroyed the Great Eye
He helps to save Sam.

Damon Walsh (10)
Swinnow Primary School

Best Friends Cinquain

Funny,
Clever, happy,
Kind and caring best friends,
She is always laughing madly,
Best mates.

Eilish Daniels (10)
Swinnow Primary School

Best Friend Cinquain

Chatting
She never stops
Every day, every week
As soon as she starts, she can't stop
Best friends.

Georgina Ford (10)
Swinnow Primary School

The Boy In Our Class

There was once a boy in our class
Who was really a big fan of grass
He went out to play
And found some hay
And made himself a hay mask.

Laura McMullen (7)
Swinnow Primary School

The Game

Today we're off to the football,
I hope the goalie can catch,
The game seemed to go on for ever,
In the end it was a good match.

Connor Hancock (11)
Swinnow Primary School

In My Teacher's Handbag

In my teacher's handbag the last time I looked was . . .
a rotten old wallet with a small hole at the side,
a ring of half snapped keys,
some mouldy sweets
a loaded gun for the children getting out of control and hostile,
a cane tough as a diamond,
a driving ticket,
some matches to set the school on fire,
a jar of snake venom,
three credit cards for opening secret rooms,
a really rotten, half-eaten pig's head for when she gets peckish,
three robins' wings,
ten pizzas,
Some bat fangs,
and cracked contact lenses.
She really is a strange teacher.

Louis Hughes (8)
Swinnow Primary School

In My Teacher's Handbag

In my teacher's handbag the last time I looked was . . .

A slimy rat's tooth,
14 dog hairs rotting away,
1 rat's leg that had no toes.
A sticky cola lolly that was stuck to a fly,
A milk carton which had been there for 2 years,
A dirty broken rubber,
Some glasses which had no lenses,
Some burnt matches which were still alight,
A rotten monkey's ears as well as an alligator's eye.

Blake Longley (9)
Swinnow Primary School

My Teacher's Handbag

In my teacher's handbag the last time I looked was . . .
a bottle of milkshake as rotten as a grate,
a broken bike's brake.
There was a worm in the pocket of her bag
wiggling like the sea,
a boot lace as white as the snow on Christmas Eve.
The last thing I saw was
a nail from a dog as sharp as a needle,
but the very last was an apple as red as a rose,
some sticky sweets from last month,
a blue pen that was leaking
and a chocolate bar wrapper as mouldy as a dead rat.

Fern Hughes (8)
Swinnow Primary School

Eleven Things Found In
The Wizard Of Oz's Pocket

A big dollop of courage,
A compass to find the wizard's home,
A map to help Dorothy find her way home,
A massive pile of hearts,
A very clever brain for the tin man,
A sparkly green wand,
A shiny crown,
A sponge to clean the crown,
A bottle of green wine,
A slimy green frog called Slippy,
And . . . some dazzling emeralds.

Tommy Cook (9)
Swinnow Primary School

Winter Haikus

Dull, winter, rainy,
Winter comes but once a year.
Christmas is joyful.

The leaves grow again,
Spring getting ready for sun,
Newborn chicks arrive.

Happy, joyful, fun,
The sun shines in the morning,
I feel so happy.

Leaves fall from the trees,
Autumn comes but once a year,
Chilly, cold, rainy.

Charlotte O'Byrne (9)
Swinnow Primary School

Season Haikus

Freezing cold winter
frosted icicles shining
frozen cars break down.

Scorching sun shining
parents cleaning the garden
flowers start to grow.

Late nights are coming,
children wearing shorts again
far too hot to sleep.

Leaves along the floor
kids playing in piles of leaves
cold, frosty weather.

Cole Harrop (9)
Swinnow Primary School

The Music Rap

Music, music everywhere!
Sing it on your own, sing it in pairs,
Musical instruments, they rock!
Guitars, drums and chime blocks.

Good songs by Justin Timberlake and Pink,
But not Robbie Williams coz he stinks!
Gonna rap to the beat,
Gonna tap my feet,
Coz music is here,
And we're gonna play it, my dear!

Music channels, songs non-stop,
Gonna rap to 50 Cents' hip hop!
Listen to it here, listen to it there,
Music is for everyone everywhere!

Alistair Ryder (9)
Swinnow Primary School

My Teacher's Handbag

In my teacher's handbag last time I looked was . . .

A green lipstick as green as the leaves,
Some frog's eyes as cool as ever.
A picture of a city as beautiful as me.
Some tablets, as strong as my dad.
Parrot feathers like a rainbow.
A pair of glasses as blue as the sea.
Twenty-two of Tommy's Tazos,
Some nail varnish as smelly as a monster's breath.
Stickers, as shiny as the sun,
Some sparkly buttons.

What a strange handbag!

Daniel Ford (8)
Swinnow Primary School

Class Time

I got to my class just on time
Running through the gates
The teacher was busy writing
She was very cross I was late.

I sat at my desk
I started to write the date
Suddenly I was frightened
I would soon find out my fate.

Thomas Royston (10)
Swinnow Primary School

Quatrain Poem

My horse runs on the track
All day long and never stops.
On the course we run and run,
Round and round all day long.
I get my horse out of its stable
So we can go running again.
For ever and ever we will go on
Because she's mine and she's very strong.

Jade Lee (10)
Swinnow Primary School

In My Teacher's Handbag Was . . .

A ruby-red lipstick for when school has finished,
A green reward card for work well done,
A lightning pen for marking our work,
A cuddly toy rabbit for class 1,
A beeping watch that she took from Jason.

Jason Firth (8)
Swinnow Primary School

All Are Cats!

Cheetah - fastest animal,
Tiger - stripy fur,
Lion - roars very loud,
Lynx - quiet as a mouse,
Puma - slinks in shadow,
Panther - climbs high,
Leopard - sharp claws.
All are cats!

Rowena Walmsley (11)
Swinnow Primary School

School Haiku

Swinnow Primary
Learning is fun at this school
Great and happy times.

Jade Thompson (9)
Swinnow Primary School

Roman Cinquain

Romans
Marching around
In their leather sandals
They had a very big empire
Conquer.

Beth Dockerty (9)
Swinnow Primary School

Fish Haiku

Fish swim in fast streams
Blowing bubbles in the sea
Twisting, swimming fish.

Ria Smith (9)
Swinnow Primary School

In My Teacher's Handbag

In my teacher's handbag the last time I looked
there was . . .
A pair of cracked glasses,
An old broken watch which won't work
Like an old grandad sitting in a chair,
Forty-four frogs for a science experiment.
A small ancient clock, covered in dead rats,
An ocean-blue lipstick,
A big slimy bogie.
A leaking container of sausage hot pot
And a cup of tea for lunch.
Twenty-two marked math's tests.
Horrid Henry doll, horrid all the time,
A Manchamp Pokémon card from my pocket,
And a fake spider to scare the girls!

Liam Strangeway (8)
Swinnow Primary School

My Teacher's Handbag

In my teacher's handbag the last time I looked
there was . . .
A packet of cough sweets as sticky as a bun,
Some false nails,
A pink mobile,
A big pile of Digimon cards.
A bird-like transformer, which I wished was mine.
Some soggy chips from the dinner hall,
Some green lipstick and
Twenty-two Tazos taken off Tommy,
Also a slimy eel, in a tube of water.

Elliot Collins (8)
Swinnow Primary School

In My Teacher's Handbag

The last time I looked in my teacher's handbag there was . . .
An ugly red pen which writes in all different colours.
Some sweaty socks which twist all different ways,
Some smelly breath freshener, that's enjoyable.
Some jiggling keys to go home.
An alarm clock made of paper,
Some alarm clock made of paper.
Some tea leaves from Sri Lanka,
A bar of melted chocolate,
A piece of bracelet, all broken up,
A fluffy scarf all red and brown.
A pair of sparkling earrings.
A sweet that's as sticky as a bun.

Lauren Sharp (8)
Swinnow Primary School

Ten Things Found In A Witch's Cauldron

A chocolate factory,
A slug for her lunch,
A hat that can speak
Some cats running and chasing a mouse.
A broomstick, all battered and bits all bent
Some potion to make trouble
A rat to keep the cat company,
Some books for when she is tired.
A spade to pick her nose with
An everlasting mint for her to chew on.

Oliver Colling (9)
Swinnow Primary School

In My Teacher's Handbag

In my teacher's handbag the last time I looked
there was . . .
A bottle of bubbling fizzing wine.
A small story book to read in case she gets bored
A pair of green glasses.
A warm, woolly, white scarf.
A witch's spell book with a wizard's wand.
Some small stones for throwing at naughty children.
A tube of lemon coloured lipstick -
A smelly pink pen
A small spider's web.
A tiny slice of half an eaten pizza,
A two month old moth,
And a rose as red as blood.

Abbie Lee (8)
Swinnow Primary School

My Teacher's Handbag

In my teacher's handbag the last time I looked was . . .

A stinky mouldy mobile,
A black lipstick for Hallowe'en.
An annoying, stupid parrot.
A mouldy poisoned apple.
A geeky green card,
Some soggy chips
A broken watch,
And . . . a stinky sharpener
Some smelly, ugly socks.

Stacy Louise Towson (8)
Swinnow Primary School

My Teacher's Handbag

In my teacher's handbag the last time I looked was . . .

A dying rat,
Grey and squeaky nails on a black, big board.
Half a pizza, big and mouldy.
An old pair of smelly socks,
An old pair of glasses made out of blue metal,
A box of matches that won't work,
A polar bear's nail for Mrs to clean her nails out with.
A key - gold and shining,
A soggy school chip - yellow and soft.
A rotten biscuit all smelly and rotten,
A smelly spare swimming kit which is still wet,
A credit card for Asda
A warm, woolly, old scarf,
And a shiny sticker for Class 4.

Danielle Middleton (8)
Swinnow Primary School

In My Teacher's Handbag

In my teacher's handbag the last time I looked
there was . . .
A disgusting old watch.
Some old, out of date tickets and money,
Some PE gear, as smelly as old socks,
A blood-red whistle with tiny crocks.
Twenty-two text books with torn pages,
A stop watch which only ticks every hour
And pictures with splattered spots of ketchup,
And some really disgusting sweaty old chips,
But if I look again, I'm sure I'll vomit.

Jared Walsh (9)
Swinnow Primary School

In My Teacher's Handbag

In my teacher's handbag the last time I looked
was a . . .
Bottle of Sunny Delight as bright as the sun.
Some sweets as sticky as Sellotape.
A pair of sparkling matches that won't work.
Two pairs of socks - black and woolly.
A rotten biscuit and a bruised apple.
A warm white scarf.
A small story book as cute as a baby.
A set of red pens for marking her work.
A broken watch which stopped at dinner time
And a broken bracelet as shiny as a star.

Billie Town (8)
Swinnow Primary School

Dog Cinquain

My dog
He is quite smart
Walks on the field with me
He is so lazy on the couch
My dog.

Luke Taylor (9)
Swinnow Primary School

About My Brother Haiku

My big, big brother
He lets me go out with him.
My brother is fun.

David Todd (10)
Swinnow Primary School

Family Reunion

Screaming babies
That are so called
Twice removed cousins,
The Danish royalty,
Several Frenchmen
A million upon trillion
Of Irishmen singing songs
That have no end.
Cockney cousins who can't speak
(Well . . . nearly)
Girls in flouncy dresses,
Boys totally ignoring everybody
But themselves.
And Canadians who really
Are Irish.
And there I am -
In the middle of them all.
Looking totally . . .
Well, normal.

Emma Reilly (11)
Wakefield Tutorial Prep School

It Wasn't My Fault

'It wasn't my fault, Mum
I didn't do it.
It was my friend up the street,
He pinched a rubber from school,
I swear he did it.'

I'm looking at my mum
With my gloomy eyes and
She says, 'Okay, I forgive you.'

Luke Kernachan (11)
Wakefield Tutorial Prep School

I Wonder Why?

I wonder why dogs bark?
I wonder why cows give milk?
I wonder why baby goats are called kids?

I wonder why snakes hiss?
I wonder why sheep have wool?
I wonder why Dalmatians are spotty?

I wonder why cats go purr?
I wonder why elephants are big?
I wonder why frogs hop?

I wonder why I wonder?
Hmm!

Sophie Walker (9)
Wakefield Tutorial Prep School

The Kickbox Man

Kick! Punch! Kick! Punch!
Goes the kickbox man.
Everybody is scared
Of the kickbox man.

He's big and tall
With a long, black belt.
A hook kick to the head
And a side kick to the body.

If ever you see the kickbox man
Run away and hide!

Jacob Atkinson (8)
Wakefield Tutorial Prep School

I Would Rather . . .

I would rather . . .
Kiss a witch with a big, green, hairy spot.
Live in a bin with a smelly banana skin
And a smelly sock.
Kiss a gorilla with a big fat mole on his nose
Like a vampire that sucks up all my blood.
Sleep with my grandma's pants on my head.
Sleep with an octopus and kiss him
When I go to bed.
Be naughty and scare people away with a grizzly bear.

Than . . .
Live with the naughtiest boy in my class for one day.

Hannah Brown (7)
Wakefield Tutorial Prep School

I Wonder Why?

I wonder why
People die?
Miss cries?
Harry likes dinosaurs?
Snails are slow?
Po is red?
I grow?
Jacob eats mushrooms?
Go on holiday?
Miss always has the same watch every day?
Troy likes rugby?

Lauren Jade Dungworth (8)
Wakefield Tutorial Prep School

Ten Dancing Elephants

Ten dancing elephants jumping on balloons,
One jumped through the floorboards,
Then there were nine.

Nine dancing elephants doing the cancan,
One kicked his leg too high
Then there were eight.

Eight dancing elephants reading funny poems,
One didn't know how to read
Then there were seven.

Seven dancing elephants kick-boxing on a stage,
One got knocked out
Then there were six.

Six dancing elephants learning how to dive,
One did a bellyflop
Then there were five.

Five dancing elephants learning how to smell
One smelt smoke
Then there were four.

Four dancing elephants in the sea,
One was attacked by a shark,
Then there were three.

Three dancing elephants swimming in a pool,
One was drowned by his brother
Then there were two.

Two dancing elephants relaxing in the sun,
One got sunburnt by the heat,
Then there was one.

One dancing elephant at a space station,
Got a rocket to Mars,
And was never seen again.

Imogen Wade (8)
Wakefield Tutorial Prep School

's Only February You Know!

What's happening to the weather?
The sun shone brightly today,
It didn't rain or snow,
So out I went to play.

Last year's leaves,
Are still on the ground.
On the trees
This year's leaves can be found
And it's only February, you know!

Shop's shelves are filled with eggs,
This gets earlier every year!
There are lots of eggs to choose,
This makes the children cheer!

Gone are the dark and cold mornings,
They're replaced by the birds,
Singing their favourite tunes,
Without the words.

When I come home from school,
The dark nights have disappeared
And I can play out till after tea.
Still it's only February, you know!

Is there something we should know?
Because the seasons,
Seem to be changing.
Would someone tell the weather . . .
It's only February, you know!

Melissa Hirst (10)
Wakefield Tutorial Prep School

I Wonder Why?

Elephants are so *big*?
Birds fly in the sky?
We have to go to school?
Knights wear armour?
Jesus got gold and frankincense and myrrh?
My teacher is so pretty?
The President is so unpopular?
Some bad people take drugs and drink too much alcohol?
Judges slam their hammer down?
Spacemen walk on the moon?

Joseph Elliott (7)
Wakefield Tutorial Prep School

The Dinosaurs

Stomp! Chomp! Stomp! Chomp!
A dinosaur stomps!
T-rex with blood dribbling
Raptors nibbling
Ankylasaurus stomping and chomping
Leaves and peas.
Stomp! Chomp! Stomp! Chomp!
A dinosaur stomps!

Harry Gavaghan (7)
Wakefield Tutorial Prep School

Who Is There?

Who is there when I say goodnight?
Who is there when I turn off the light?
Who is there when I fall in a hole?
Who is there when I stole a bowl?
Who is there when I hold the batton?
Who is there when I say, 'Hands on!'?
Who is there when I pick up the phone?
Who is there when I steal the dog's bone?
Who is there when I shout out, 'Boo!'?
Who is there when I'm on the loo?
Who is there when I tell a joke?
Who is there when I swim breaststroke?

Jessica Clegg (9)
Wakefield Tutorial Prep School

I Like To See

I like to see . . .
Tractors working in the fields,
Sheep having lambs,
Chickens having chicks.
Horses galloping round the fields,
Pigs oinking in the pigsty.
Cows mooing in the sheds,
Dogs barking in their kennels.

James Rathmell (7)
Wakefield Tutorial Prep School

I Can't Help It

I can't help it if I drop a bottle of ink,
I can't help it if my ring goes down the sink.
I can't help it if I fall in the snow.
It's not my fault the stain on my shirt won't go.

I can't help it if my homework falls in a puddle,
I can't help it if I get my poem in a muddle.
I can't help it if I don't like reading much,
It's not my fault that I broke my gran's crutch.

I can't help it if my hamster escapes,
I can't help it if I stand on my mum's grapes.
It's not my fault everyone torments me,
I want to be normal, can't you see?

Felicia Lauren Doubell (10)
Wakefield Tutorial Prep School

Travelling Creepy-Crawlies

A snail left a trail on the way to Sweden
A spider walked all the way to Spain.
A bug crawled all the way to Brazil,
A centipede jumped all the way to Canada,
A worm wriggled all the way to Washington DC.
A beetle flew all the way to Brisbane
A slug slivered all the way to Switzerland.
An army of ants marched all the way to Argentina.

Alexandros Bottonis (7)
Wakefield Tutorial Prep School